SimpleLaw
Texas Divorce

L. Keith Martinson
Attorney at Law
Ft. Worth, Texas

Published by
SimpleLaw, Inc.

"SimpleLaw
Texas Divorce"
(version 20-01-3)

Publisher:
SimpleLaw, Inc.®
P.O. Box 8, Bridgeport, TX 76426
940-575-2731 or 800-585-8481
www.simplelaw.com
e-mail: support@simplelaw.com

WARNING

**Do not use the pre-printed, fill-in-the-blank forms unless you meet the following requirements.
When you file for your divorce, you or your spouse must have been a resident of Texas for the
last 6 months and a resident of the county where you are going to file for the divorce for the
last 90 days; the wife cannot be pregnant; neither spouse can be in bankruptcy; and, you are
not going to split either spouse's retirement benefits. If you are going to split one or both of the
spouse's retirement benefits, or if the Texas Attorney General is involved in your case, or if a
protective order has been issued against you or your spouse, you must use our CD-ROM
software. If you purchased our form book without the CD-ROM software, you may call us at
940-575-2731 or 800-585-8481 and place your order or visit our web site at
"www.simplelaw.com".**

*BE SURE TO REGISTER YOUR PURCHASE TO BE
ELIGIBLE FOR THE LATEST UPDATES.*

This product is not a substitute for
the advice of an attorney.

About the Author
L. Keith Martinson, Attorney at Law

L. Keith Martinson, author of SimpleLaw Texas Divorce, SimpleLaw Texas Name Change, SimpleLaw Texas Wills & Trusts, and SimpleLaw Texas General Forms, and who is the President of SimpleLaw, Inc., is a Family Law Attorney currently practicing in Fort Worth, Texas.

A graduate of Texas Tech University School of Law and licensed to practice law by the Supreme Court of the State of Texas since 1986, Mr. Martinson is well-respected and known for his positive achievements in the legal field. He also understands the need for Texas specific do-it-yourself products.

Working with the Texas courts on a daily basis allows Mr. Martinson to keep SimpleLaw, Inc.'s Software & Form Books up-to-date with Texas laws.

Mr. Martinson works diligently at making sure SimpleLaw, Inc.'s Software & Form Books provide the documents and instructions that result in accurate, affordable, and complete legal work for self-representation in Texas.

Prior to entering the legal profession Mr. Martinson obtained his Associate's Degree from American River College in Sacramento, CA, his Bachelor's Degree from Minot State College in Minot, ND, and completed 2 years of post-graduate studies at the Criminal Justice Institute at Sam Houston State University in Huntsville, TX. He worked extensively with the criminal justice system in Texas before opening his Family Law practice. His involvement included several years as a Texas State Parole Officer in Houston and a Felony Adult Probation Officer in Fort Worth.

In addition to practicing law Mr. Martinson authored a series of audio tapes entitled Understanding the Law. This series, which was widely distributed to libraries in Texas as well as among his many clients, included practical information on the legal aspects of Divorce, Bankruptcy, Landlord/Tenant Relationships, Collections, and several other topics. In 1997 he authored his first work for SimpleLaw, Inc. entitled SimpleLaw Texas Divorce. Over the next several years he added various other form books and software titles to his list with SimpleLaw, Inc. including those titles listed above.

FREE UPDATES

After you have loaded your CD-ROM, please go to our website at **www.simplelaw.com** and **download any updates to the SimpleLaw Texas Divorce Q & A version that are posted**. Updating this program insures that you have the most recent legal language under statute.

Just follow the instructions on the website to download your update. You will have to know where you installed your program to obtain the update. This, by default, is C:\SLTXDIV. If you did not use the default installation path, you will need to install the updates in the path that you chose.

If you are using any of the **Divorce Wordpad Template versions**, you must update these by filling out the REGISTRATION FORM on the next page and mailing it to SimpleLaw, Inc., P.O. Box 8, Bridgeport, TX 76426 along with a self-addressed envelope with 3 first class postage stamps affixed. Be sure to indicate which template you want updated.

If you do not have an Internet account, you may order the Free update for the Divorce Q & A version via diskette for a nominal handling fee. Contact our Sales Department at 940-575-2731.

Free updates are available for six months after you install the program. If you need an extension, you may order one from SimpleLaw at www.simplelaw.com or 940-575-2731.

Please contact us for any other legal software you may need. Thank you for choosing SimpleLaw.

NOTICE

1. Note the page numbers for the following forms are located in the upper left corner.

2. Please read all instructions completely and carefully.

3. Register your purchase using this page.

REGISTRATION FORM (20-01-3)

Register your copy of SimpleLaw Texas Divorce so that we can inform you of any changes that may have been made to Texas divorce law since your forms were published. Updates for the pre-printed, fill-in-the-blank forms and the CD-ROM Wordpad versions are free for six months from the date of purchase to those who register within 30 days of purchase and provide proof of purchase by enclosing your original sales receipt or a true copy of your sales receipt with the form below. Updates for the CD-ROM software are free off our website for the first six months to those who register online within 30 days of purchase. __Be sure to include a self-addressed envelope with three (3) first class postage stamps affixed.__ *Updates on CD-ROM are free (shipping & handling charges of $8.95 apply).*

*NAME*_____

*ADDRESS*_____

*CITY, STATE, ZIP*_____

TELEPHONE NUMBER (_____)_____ *PURCHASE DATE*_____

*STORE WHERE PURCHASED*_____ *CITY*_____

E-MAIL ADDRESS _____

PLEASE CHECK THE VERSIONS THAT YOU WISH TO UPDATE:

_____ **DIVORCE WORDPAD TEMPLATE - NO CHILDREN**

_____ **DIVORCE WORDPAD TEMPLATE - ONE CHILD**

_____ **DIVORCE WORDPAD TEMPLATE - 2 OR MORE CHILDREN**

SimpleLaw, Inc., PO Box 8, Bridgeport, TX 76426

<u>NOTICE</u>

THERE IS ONLY ONE WAY TO INSTALL THIS SOFTWARE AND HAVE IT WORK CORRECTLY.

YOU MUST FOLLOW THE INSTRUCTIONS EXACTLY AS SET FORTH ON THE NEXT PAGE.

YOU MUST ALSO UPDATE YOUR PROGRAM FROM OUR WEB SITE AT **WWW.SIMPLELAW.COM**

YOUR <u>CD</u> <u>KEY</u> <u>NUMBER</u> (PASSWORD) IS LOCATED AT THE BOTTOM OF THE "HOW TO INSTALL" PAGE.

HOW TO INSTALL YOUR SIMPLELAW TEXAS DIVORCE PROGRAM

1. Insert the CD ROM into the CD Drive.

2. Wait for the AutoMenu to come up. If, after 1 minute, the AutoMenu does not appear, type S:Setup.exe where S: is your CD drive letter.

3. Click Texas Legal Products.

4. Click Texas Divorce Products.

5. Click on the Texas Divorce Q&A, Version 2.x Program.

6. Read and Agree to the License Agreement. If you do not accept, the program will not install on your hard drive.

7. Read the instructions and click Next.

8. **Do not change the default directory.** The program must be installed in C:\TXSLDIV. Click Next.

9. Click Next.

10. Wait for the program to install. Click Finish.

11. You will be asked to restart your computer after the installation is complete. Click OK.

12. After your machine reboots, there will be an Icon on your desktop. There will also be a SimpleLaw Texas Divorce Program group added under Programs.

13. Click the Texas Uncontest...Icon (or click Start, then click Programs, then click SimpleLaw Texas Divorce, and then click Texas Uncontested Divorce).

14. You will be asked for a 5 digit CD key. The CD Key Number for

- **SimpleLaw Texas Divorce Q&A, Version 2.x is 76226**

15. Click the Hand to continue.

16. Read the next several screens. These instructions explain how to use some of the features in the SimpleLaw Texas Divorce Program. Click Next after you have finished reading or completing any steps. On the final instruction you will be asked to Print the Beginning Help. Your printer should be on-line and ready to print. This Help includes additional instructions and worksheets to gather your data. Follow the on-screen instructions.

<u>Important Note</u>

If you get a **Write Conflict**, you MUST use the **Save Record** button to continue. You will get a **Write Conflict** on the **Who is Filing for Divorce** screen. If you do not use the **Save Record**, you will get several additional errors and the program will not work correctly. If you did not use the **Save Record** the first time, do it the second time that you get the conflict notice.

If you prefer to use a fill-in-the-blank version of the divorce program rather than the question and answer version as listed above, please use the following Passwords to access the appropriate divorce programs.

- SimpleLaw Texas Divorce WordPad Template, No Children ... **76534**

- SimpleLaw Texas Divorce WordPad Template, 1 Child ... **87654**

- SimpleLaw Texas Divorce WordPad Template, 2 or more Children ... **64332**

HOW THE DIVORCE PROGRAM WORKS

This interactive program utilizes the "interview" process wherein the program simply asks you a series of questions. Your responses to those questions are automatically inserted into the legal documents you need for your specific case for printing. This program also automatically calculates child support amounts based upon your answers to the questions asked. All documents may be edited after you have completed the interview process. This ensures that your divorce is tailored to your specific circumstances. Please note, however, that all divorce agreements are subject to the approval of the Court.

A WORD ABOUT CLOSING DOCUMENTS

Most divorce cases contain property or debts that were divided in the Final Decree of Divorce. In order to implement the actual division of this property or debts, "closing documents" are normally necessary. Examples of closing documents are "deeds" which transfer or end interests in real estate, "powers of attorney" which allow one to perform an act for another such as transferring title to an automobile, and "assignments" which allow transfers of money in accounts from one name to another. Please review the next three pages for more information.

Dear SimpleLaw Customer,

Thank you for purchasing our SimpleLaw product.

We want to let you know that with almost every divorce, "Closing Documents" are necessary as well as helpful. A Deed for Transferring Ownership in Real Estate will most likely be required by your mortgage company. A Special Power of Attorney is usually necessary in obtaining a new title to your motor vehicle. The Insurance Letter and Mortgage Letter are in ready form, also, to keep your finishing tasks simple and speedy.

We have included a printout of the specific documents that are available with a description of each one. We urge you and/or your spouse to sign all of the necessary documents either before the divorce is actually finalized or shortly thereafter. Don't make the mistake of you and your ex-spouse not signing the correct documents even after your divorce is complete.

SimpleLaw, Inc. now offers all of the listed documents on our "Closing Documents" program. The program is not on sale in the retail stores. The "Closing Documents" are available as either fill-in-the-blank forms or on CD-ROM.

The cost is $14.95 plus shipping, handling, and tax. Visa, MasterCard, Discover, American Express and e-checks are accepted.

Please give us a call or visit our web site to place your order.

SimpleLaw, Inc.
P.O. Box 8
Bridgeport, TX 76426
940-575-2731
1-800-585-8481
www.simplelaw.com

Closing Documents

Assignment of Interest — Use this form to *transfer* any interest you or your ex-spouse may have in any type of property, *except* real property and personal property that has a "title of ownership." Real Property consists of land and mineral rights but not mobile homes. Personal property that has a "title of ownership" includes such things as mobile homes, motor vehicles, trailers, boats, motorcycles, jet skis, stocks, bonds, and the like. This form should be used for personal property transfers such as bank accounts, club memberships, and the like.

Irrevocable Bond Power of Attorney — Use this form to transfer any interest you or your ex-spouse may have in corporate bonds, not U.S. Savings Bonds.

Be sure to contact a securities representative such as a stockbroker or someone who works for a company like Edward Jones & Co. before you sign this form. It is usually necessary that this form be signed in the presence of a security representative, not a notary public.

Insurance Letter — Send this form letter to the life insurance company to request the necessary forms to change the presently listed beneficiary to someone else.

Automobile Lease Assignment — Use this form to transfer any interest you or your ex-spouse may have in a motor vehicle lease agreement.

Mortgage Letter — Send this form letter to the mortgage company that is holding the note on any real property that you or your ex-spouse may have an interest in. This form allows the mortgage company to transfer interests in any monies held in escrow to pay taxes, insurance or the like from one ex-spouse to the other.

Quit Claim Deed — Have your ex-spouse sign this form to keep the title to any real property or land that you owned before you married or that you inherited during your marriage or that was given to you as a gift during your marriage clear of any claims of that ex-spouse. After this form has been signed in the presence of a notary public it needs to be filed with the County Clerk in the county where the land is located.

Special Power of Attorney to Transfer Motor Vehicle — Use this form to get a new title to a motor vehicle that has either just your ex-spouse's name on the title of ownership or has both your name and your ex-spouse's name on the title of ownership. After this form has been signed in the presence of a notary public by the spouse who is giving up his or her interest in the motor vehicle, it must be presented to the proper licensing authority in your county to transfer title of ownership.

Special Warranty Deed — You would sign this form to transfer your ownership interest in any real property, land or mineral rights that you and your ex-spouse acquired during your marriage to your ex-spouse. Your ex-spouse would sign this form to transfer his or her ownership interest in that real property, land or mineral rights to you. Be sure that this form is signed in the presence of a notary public. After it has been properly signed, it needs to be filed with the County Clerk in the county where the real property, land or mineral rights is located.

Irrevocable Stock Power of Attorney — Use this form to transfer any interest you or your ex-spouse may have in corporate stock.

Be sure to contact a securities representative such as a stockbroker or someone who works for a company like Edward Jones & Co. before you sign this form, It is usually necessary that this form be signed in the presence of a security representative, not a notary public.

Utility Deposits Assignment — Use this form to transfer any interest you or your ex-spouse may have in any deposits that either of you had to pay to any utility companies before they would give you service. Such utility companies may include the electric company, telephone company, gas company, cable television company, satellite television company, trash pickup company, and the like.

General Warranty Deed — You or your ex-spouse usually sign this form to transfer ownership in any real property, land or mineral rights that you or your ex-spouse acquired before or during your marriage, to a third party, not to you or your ex-spouse. Be sure that this form is signed in the presence of a notary public. After it has been properly signed, it needs to be filed with the County Clerk in the county where the real property, land or mineral rights is located.

Products List - *SimpleLaw, Inc.*

**You are welcome to order directly from us by calling 800-585-8481
or visiting our web site at www.simplelaw.com
or you may purchase through your local retail bookstore.**

The prices listed do not include shipping, handling & sales tax.

SimpleLaw TEXAS Divorce Form Book

Fill in the blank forms. For divorce with and without children; ISBN 1-893983-10-2: *$19.95*

SimpleLaw TEXAS Divorce CD-ROM

Interactive software prints all forms, procedures and testimony for a divorce with or without children; *$29.95*

SimpleLaw TEXAS Divorce Form Book with CD-ROM

Buy both the form book and the CD-ROM at the same time and **save $10**; ISBN 1-893983-11-0: *$39.95*

SimpleLaw TEXAS Wills & Trusts Form Book

Fill in the blank forms; includes Wills, Living Wills, Powers of Attorney, and 13 miscellaneous forms; ISBN 0-9661181-2-X: *$19.95*

SimpleLaw TEXAS Wills & Trusts CD-ROM

Interactive software includes Wills, Living Wills, Powers of Attorney, and 13 miscellaneous forms; *$29.95*

SimpleLaw TEXAS Wills & Trusts Form Book with CD-ROM

Buy both the form book and the CD-ROM at the same time and **save $10**; *$39.95*

SimpleLaw TEXAS Name Change Form Book

Fill in the blank forms for adult <u>or</u> child. Form book also contains 10 miscellaneous forms including Statutory Durable Power of Attorney, Authorization to Consent to Medical Treatment of a Minor & Promissory Note; ISBN 0-9661181-5-4: *$19.95*

SimpleLaw TEXAS Name Change CD-ROM

Interactive software prints all forms, procedures and testimony for an adult <u>or</u> child name change; *$29.95*

SimpleLaw TEXAS Name Change Form Book with CD-ROM

Buy both the form book and the CD-ROM at the same time and **save $10**; *$39.95*

SimpleLaw TEXAS General Forms Form Book - Vol. I

> Includes 25 fill in the blank forms including Lease Agreement, Affidavit, Medical Authorization Form, Five different Deeds; Promissory Note, Power of Attorney, and more; ISBN 1-893983-06-4: *$19.95*

SimpleLaw TEXAS General Forms CD-ROM - Vol. I

> Includes 42 fill in the blank forms including Lease Agreement, Affidavit, Medical Authorization Form, Five different Deeds; Promissory Note, Power of Attorney, Living Wills, Declaration of Guardian, Mechanic's Lien and more; *$29.95*

SimpleLaw TEXAS General Forms Vol. I Form Book with CD-ROM

> Buy both the form book and the CD-ROM at the same time and **save $10**; *$39.95*

SimpleLaw TEXAS Divorce Closing Documents CD-ROM or Paper Forms

> Contains 11 forms including three Powers of Attorney, three Deeds, three Assignments and two letters; *$14.95*

SimpleLaw TEXAS Modifications Software

> Now you can modify your child support without hiring an attorney. Our software contains all the forms, instructions, and testimony necessary to increase or decrease your child support payments. (Available in MicroSoft Word version); *$29.95*

*   **We also have numerous individual and business forms in MicroSoft® Word® and WordPerfect® formats on 3.5 inch floppy disk or in paper, fill-in-the-blank format. Call 800-585-8481 with your form request.**

TABLE OF CONTENTS

INTRODUCTION

The first thing you probably noticed about this book was that it was specifically designed for doing your own divorce in the State of Texas. That was exactly my intention when I conceived the idea for this book in 1996; and that is exactly what the publishers attempted to convey to you before you purchased this book. I have been practicing Family Law (divorces, adoptions, name changes, and the like) in the State of Texas since 1986. Having been an active divorce attorney in Tarrant County (Ft. Worth area) since I became licensed to practice law by the Supreme Court of the State of Texas and a member of the State Bar of Texas, I consulted with numerous people each year who wanted to do their own divorce. Unfortunately these individuals were attempting to use divorce self-help products that were written in other states, usually by out-of-state attorneys. While the concept was usable, generally the end product was not. By the time I was paid my usual legal fees for straightening out the paperwork that had been prepared by the person, that person could have hired me to complete the divorce for them from start to finish. Ten years later I decided it was time to do something for Texans who wanted to complete their own divorce. My first self-help divorce guide, an interactive software program, was published by *SimpleLaw, Inc.* in 1997. That was followed in 1998 by my first form book. That first version of the software as well as the form book has been modified through the years as necessary due to legislative changes in the divorce laws. This form book and the divorce software on CD-ROM are the latest and most comprehensive versions to date.

The Form Book

This divorce form book is designed for those of you who wish to complete your own divorce without the assistance of an attorney. Being a form book, it is naturally somewhat limited in its parameters. This form book will, however, allow you to:

- Complete your divorce even if you have children

- Designate the spouses as conservators of the child or children

- Establish visitation using standard Texas guidelines

- Establish child support obligations

- Establish health insurance obligations for the child or children

- Award property, both real and personal, to each spouse

- Award debts to each spouse

- Change the wife's name if she desires

The CD-ROM Interactive Software

The divorce software on CD-ROM has many more options available to you and your spouse. Instead of typing the information on the forms provided in the form book, the software version is interactive in that you simply respond to prompted questions. The software figures out what forms you need and even prints complete instructions for the procedure you need to follow as well as your court testimony. The software is also fully editable thereby allowing you to customize the standardized language in the divorce forms to fit your particular situation. While this is not recommended without the direct assistance of a licensed attorney of your choice, this feature has been a requested option by previous purchasers of the software since 1997. In addition to allowing you to accomplish all of the features in the form book version, the CD-ROM software version also allows you to:

- Customize the language in the divorce forms to suit your particular situation

- Divide retirement benefits between the spouses

- Provide for provisions if the Texas Attorney General is involved in your case

- Provide for provisions if a protective order is pending or has been issued in your case

Both the form book and the interactive software come with free updates for 6 months from the date of purchase as long as you register your purchase as instructed by the publisher. You may also visit the publisher's web site at **www.simplelaw.com** for other form books and software or e-mail the publisher if you should have any questions about the product or products you purchased.

Be sure to read through the book to get a feeling of what will be required of you before you just "jump right in." The procedures must be followed correctly in order for you to complete your divorce without problems.

1

How To Use This Book

It is very important that you read through this book from beginning to end before you do anything else. It has been my experience that most mistakes are made because the instructions were not read. Please do not just "begin" working on your divorce by flipping to the first page that you think applies to your situation and begin typing. This book is purposefully divided into sections in an effort to make doing your own divorce easier for you from a paperwork and procedural perspective. In addition to the **Introduction**, which I sincerely hope you have already read, we have **Chapters** that contain invaluable information as well as necessary forms. The **Table of Contents** should assist you in locating key information and forms. **Appendix A** contains a form not-so-delicately known as a Pauper's Affidavit. This affidavit may allow you to file for your divorce without paying any filing fees if you qualify. **Appendix B** contains a complete list of all the District Clerks along with their addresses and telephone numbers. **Appendix C** contains a compilation of relevant Texas Family Code sections. The Texas Family Code is the set of laws that governs the marriage relationship as well as any subsequent dissolution of that marriage.

The Chapters

The form book is divided into chapters in an effort to make doing your own divorce easier for you from a paperwork perspective. This Chapter 1 explains how to use this book to your best advantage. Chapter 2 discusses the legal procedure for getting married in Texas, the Annulment, Having a Marriage Declared Void, and Divorce. Chapter 3 talks about the divorce process, property rights, maintenance (alimony), debts, and children of the marriage. Chapters 4 and 5 contain the instructions, procedures and forms for your divorce with no children. Chapters 6 and 7 contain the instructions, procedures and forms for your divorce with children.

The Table of Contents

This section of the book should assist you in quickly and easily locating the necessary information and forms that are required for you to prepare your own divorce.

The Appendixes

Appendix A will give you the necessary information and form to file for your divorce if you cannot afford the filing fees. Appendix B is a complete list of the District Clerks in Texas along with their addresses and telephone numbers. Appendix C is a compilation of relevant portions of the Texas Family Code for your reference.

2

The Marriage

Let me start by saying that Section 1.101 of the Texas Family Code states that "..., every marriage entered into in this state is presumed to be valid unless expressly made void by ..." by dissolution "...or unless expressly made voidable...and annulled..." As such there are several ways to "end" a marriage relationship. These include Annulment, Having a Marriage Declared Void, and Divorce.

The Marriage Procedure

In general terms, in the State of Texas, you must have completed several steps before you were allowed to marry. These steps included appearing before the county clerk to obtain a marriage license. This procedure included showing the clerk proof of identity and age, filling out a proscribed form and taking an oath. Once the marriage license was issued by the clerk, you must have waited at least 72 hours, but no longer than 30 days, to marry. There are exceptions to these general rules, but I will not attempt to get into all the exceptions that can occur. After your marriage ceremony, the marriage license was returned to the clerk by the person who married you. It was then returned to you and your spouse.

Annulment

In order to be eligible for an annulment one of several situations must exist. These are specifically outlined in Chapter 6, Subchapter B of the Texas Family Code. These include certain situations involving a spouse being under the age of 14 years, a spouse being between 14 and 18 years of age, a spouse being under the influence of alcohol or narcotics at the time of the marriage, impotency, fraud, duress, force, mental incompetency, concealed divorce, and getting married less than 72 hours after the issuance of the marriage license. If you believe you fit under any of these provisions and may qualify for an annulment, you should consult with a licensed attorney of your choice for legal advice.

Having a Marriage Declared Void

You may be eligible to have your marriage declared void if the marrige consists of spouses who are too closely related or if one of the spouses was already married when the present marriage took place. These are specifically outlined in Chapter 6, Subchapter C of the Texas Family Code. If you believe you fit under either of these provisions and may qualify for a void marriage, you should consult with a licensed attorney of your choice for legal advice.

Divorce

Chapter 6, Subchapter A of the Texas Family Code outlines the grounds for divorce, which is sometimes referred to as dissolution of a marriage. These grounds include insupportability, cruelty, adultery, conviction of a felony, abandonment, living apart, and confinement in a mental hospital.

The "no fault" ground of insupportability is often compared to the California ground known as irreconcilable differences. This insupportability ground in Texas allows a court to divorce the spouses "...if the marriage has become insupportable because of discord or conflict of personalities that destroys the legitimate ends of the marital relationship and prevents any reasonable expectation of reconciliation." This is the single most common ground used for the granting of a divorce in this state.

Cruelty may be used to have a divorce granted "...in favor of one spouse if the other spouse is guilty of cruel treatment toward the complaining spouse of a nature that renders further living together insupportable." Until 1970, this was the most common ground for divorce in Texas.

Adultery, which has been defined as voluntary sexual intercourse between a married man and someone other than his wife or between a married woman and someone other than her husband, is grounds for divorce in Texas.

"The court may grant a divorce in favor of one spouse if during the marriage the other spouse has been convicted of a felony, has been imprisoned for at least one year in the state penitentiary, a federal penitentiary, or the penitentiary of another state, and has not been pardoned."

When one spouse has left the other spouse with the intention of abandonment and that spouse has remained away for at least one year, the court may grant a divorce.

The court may also grant a divorce "...if the spouses have lived apart without cohabitation for at least three years."

This book will only address the issue of insupportability as it deals with your divorce situation. Should you feel a need to assert any of the other grounds for a divorce, please consult with a licensed attorney of your choice.

3

The Divorce

A single divorce lawsuit can potentially contain three lawsuits in one. First is the dissolution of the marriage. The second is to divide the property. And the third is a suit involving the children, if any. This book covers all three situations but necessarily is limited by available space. The divorce CD-ROM software, however, allows you to make provisions for property division and child custody, visitation and support that are beyond the scope of this form book.

A divorce necessarily involves the drafting and filing of several documents. The initial document is the Original Petition for Divorce. This document contains information about the parties, their marriage, their children, and any requests for a change of name. Other documents include the Waiver of Citation, the Final Decree of Divorce, and the Employer's Order to Withhold Earnings for Child Support (if applicable in your situation). The Waiver of Citation is a formal acknowledgment by your spouse to the court that he or she knows a divorce suit has been filed, that he or she has received a copy of the Original Petition for Divorce and understands it. The Final Decree of Divorce sets forth your agreement with your spouse concerning all your property and debts and, if you have children, the parties' rights and responsibilities regarding the children. The

Employer's Order to Withhold Earnings for Child Support is an order to the employer of the spouse who is going to pay child support.

Basic Information About Doing Your Own Divorce

While it would not be uncommon for an attorney to charge you several hundreds of dollars in legal fees **plus** costs of court to represent you in a divorce suit, you can expect to spend considerably less if you do it yourself. We know you bought this form book, so let's start with the $20 retail price ($40 if you bought the form book with the CD-ROM). Add to that the costs of court, sometimes referred to as the filing fee, in the approximate amount of $180. These costs of court will vary from county to county. Since you will necessarily have to copy the forms in this book as well as provide additional duplicate copies when you go to court, you can expect to spend about $7.00 for copies for a divorce with no children and about $14.00 for copies for a divorce with children. This would total about $207.00 if you use the form book and have no children to $234.00 if you use the form book with the CD-ROM and have children. Bear in mind that there may be other costs associated with the divorce including, but not limited to, fees to the child support office in your county.

The **minimum** time to obtain a divorce in the State of Texas is sixty-one days. Under section 6.702 of the Texas Family Code, "The court may not grant a divorce before the 60th day after the date the suit was filed."

Under section 6.706 of the Texas Family Code, either spouse may ask the court to change his or her name "...to a name **previously** used by the party...".

Remarriage in Texas is prohibited under section 6.801 of the Texas Family Code for a period of 30 days after the divorce is granted. Specifically the code states "...neither party to a divorce may marry a third party before the 31st day after the date the divorce is decreed." The exception is that you may remarry your former spouse in this divorce at any time. Section 6.802 allows for a judicial waiver of the prohibition against remarriage. It states in part "For good cause shown the court may waive the prohibition against remarriage provided by this subchapter as to either or both spouses...".

If you and your spouse decide to reconcile after you have filed for the divorce, you may simply not do anything else. In time the divorce suit that was filed will be dismissed by the court. If you file for divorce, reconcile, then split up again and decide to proceed with the divorce **after** it has been dismissed by the court, you simply start all over again as if you had never filed the first divorce lawsuit. If you file for divorce, reconcile, then split up again and decide to proceed with the divorce **before** it has been dismissed by the court, you should consult with a licensed attorney of your choice as to how best to proceed.

If the wife is pregnant, a divorce can, in some limited circumstances, still be granted. This situation is, however, beyond the scope of both this form book and the CD-ROM software version. You should consult a licensed attorney of your choice.

If the attorney general of the state of Texas has been involved in your marriage through previous court proceedings, you may still be able to use the CD-ROM version of this book but not this form book. Due to the innumerable variations that may exist due to attorney general involvement, even the CD-ROM software may not be enough to address all the specific situations that may be encountered. The best way to proceed, if you decide to use the software version of this product, is to notify the attorney general of the pending divorce suit by sending them a copy of the original petition for divorce and asking them what specific language they will require in the final decree of divorce.

Property Rights of the Parties

In Texas there are two types of property involved in divorces. The first is separate property. Separate property under section 3.001 of the Texas Family Code is defined as "(1) property owned or claimed by the spouse before marriage; (2) the property acquired by the spouse during marriage by gift, devise, or descent; and (3) the recovery for personal injuries sustained by the spouse during marriage, except any recovery for loss of earning capacity during marriage."

Section 3.002 defines community property as consisting "of the property, other than separate property, acquired by either spouse during marriage."

Family code section 7.001 provides "In a decree of divorce, ..." the court shall order a division of the estate of the parties in a manner that the court deems just and right,..." This section provides the foundation for you and your spouse to agree on a division of your property in your divorce. In your testimony when you go to court to "prove up", or finish, your divorce, you will testify that the division of property is "fair, just and equitable" for both of you. Usually the court will accept this without question or further testimony from you. On occasion you will find the presiding judge who will want to know more specifics. Just answer this judge's questions honestly and you should have no problem.

Maintenance (Otherwise Known as Alimony)

Chapter 8 of the Texas Family Code outlines the maintenance in this state. You may refer to that chapter in Appendix C of this book for specific language. In a nutshell maintenance means an award in a suit for dissolution of a marriage of periodic payments from the future income of one spouse for the support of the other spouse. Factors in determining maintenance are set forth in section 8.003 with the amount of maintenance capped at 20% of the paying spouse's average monthly gross income or $2,500, whichever is less. The maintenance **may not** be ordered for more than 3 years after the date of the divorce order and **must** terminate on the death of either party or on the remarriage of the party receiving maintenance. The maintenance **may** end if the party receiving the maintenance cohabits with another person in a permanent place of abode on a continuing, conjugal basis.

Debts

Debts may be divided in any manner as the parties agree. As a general rule, if you get the property, you get the debt associated with it. The single most common problem with debt division is when one spouse incurs the debt and the other spouse agrees to pay it after divorce. Even if you put in the Final Decree of Divorce that your spouse is going to pay a debt in your name, that does not necessarily mean that he or she will. Whatever your agreement, the party who incurred the debt will remain the responsible party in the eyes of the creditor. Should your spouse fail to make the payment as agreed, the creditor may come looking to you for the money.

Another problem with debt division arises when real estate is involved. If you and your spouse bought a house or other real estate during the marriage and it was financed in both of your names, usually that debt will remain in both of your names after the divorce unless the real estate is either refinanced by one of the parties or is sold to a third party. Just because you deed (give) the real estate to the other party as a part of the divorce, your name will not automatically be removed from the underlying note for the debt. Please contact your mortgage company for specific information about the debt in the event of a divorce.

If you and your spouse owe back taxes, special rules and provisions may apply. Please consult with a licensed tax attorney before you complete your divorce.

Children

A divorce lawsuit necessarily contains a lawsuit involving the minor children of the marriage. Section 153.131 states "...the appointment of the parents of a child as joint managing conservators is in the best interest of a child....". This form book therefore utilizes the appointment of the parents as joint conservators in the Final Decree of Divorce. The CD-ROM version also contains the joint conservator language by default but, since it is editable, you may modify the provisions as you deem necessary. Please note that all provisions in your Final Decree of Divorce that relate to your child must be "in the best interest of your child."

Please note that "joint custody" and "shared custody" are not the same. Joint custody refers to the rights, powers, duties and obligations of the parents to the children of the marriage after the divorce. Shared custody defines the amount of time the children spend with each parent after the divorce. True shared custody means the children spend an equal amount of time with each parent after the divorce.

This form book utilizes the key aspects of the standard child visitation schedule under Chapter 153 of the Texas Family Code. The CD-ROM software uses the same provisions of Chapter 153 but, once again, since you can edit the terms and provisions in the Final Decree of Divorce, you can tailor-make your own visitation schedule pursuant to you and your spouses desires. Just remember not all visitation schedules are enforceable and that any and all provisions of your Final Decree of Divorce are subject to the approval of the court before you are divorced.

Health insurance coverage for the children is a must in all divorce cases. Chapter 154 of the Texas Family Code addresses all health insurance issues in divorce cases. This form book presumes that the non-custodial parent (the parent with whom the children do not live and who pays child support) will provide health insurance for the children after the divorce becomes final as well as pay for it. Section 154.183 states that "An amount that an obligor is required to pay for health insurance for the child: (1) is in addition to the amount that the obligor is required to pay for child support under the guidelines for child support;..." An "obligor" is a person who is obligated or mandated to pay for something, in this case child support or health insurance premiums. The CD-ROM software uses the same provisions of Chapter 154 but, once again, since you can edit the terms and provisions in the Final Decree of Divorce, you can modify the language regarding who will provide and pay for the health insurance for the children pursuant to you and your spouses desires. Just remember that any and all provisions of your Final Decree of Divorce are subject to the approval of the court before you are divorced.

Court-ordered child support, as provided for in Chapter 154 of the Texas Family Code, is usually paid by the parent with whom the children do not live. The applicable provisions of this chapter of the code are included in Appendix C for your reference. Generally speaking, however, child support is paid until the youngest child is 18 years old and has graduated from high school. Other terminating triggers include judicial emancipation of the child, the child's marriage, the child's enlistment in the armed forces, the child's death, or other order of the court. The provisions obligating a parent to provide and pay for health insurance for the children also generally terminate upon one of the above-listed events regarding child support. Please note there are special rules for disabled children and child support/health insurance obligations. If you have a child who you believe is disabled, you may want to invest in a consultation with a licensed attorney of your choice for guidelines.

Child support is generally paid by wage withholding unless waived by the parties and the court. For a waiver of child support wage withholding in the Final Decree of Divorce, you must utilize the divorce CD-ROM software. This form book does not provide for any such waiver.

The amount of child support to be paid by the non-custodial parent to the custodial parent is often a sore spot. Chapter 154, Subchapter B of the Texas Family Code sets forth the method for computing child support. Please see Appendix C for the specific language used. The use of this form book necessitates a manual calculation by you of your "net resources" as well as the amount of your child support. The CD-ROM software calculates everything for you pursuant to your answers to specific questions.

4

The Divorce with No Children

This chapter covers instructions, procedures, and court testimony for a divorce without any children of this marriage or if you have children of this marriage who are over the age of 18 years and out of high school, or are otherwise emancipated. If you had any children born to or adopted by you during this marriage who are under the age of 18 years, are still in high school, and have not otherwise been emancipated, please go to Chapter 6 for appropriate instructions and Chapter 7 for the appropriate forms.

The Instructions

Six pages of this chapter are devoted to instructions for filling out the Original Petition for Divorce, Waiver of Citation, and Final Decree of Divorce. Please follow them very carefully and be sure to double check your work. Correct spelling of the names is mandatory as is the description of property and identification of various accounts.

What Do I Do With These Forms Now?

The two pages that follow the instructions walk you through the procedure of copying and filing with the court clerk. Pay special attention to the order of the procedure and be sure you follow it very carefully. The Original Petition for Divorce **must** be filed with the clerk's office **before** you have your spouse sign the Waiver of Citation. Any other sequence will render the Waiver of Citation void forcing you to have it signed a second time by your spouse.

The Courtroom Testimony

The last two pages of this chapter consist of your courtroom testimony. These are the "magic words" that make all your efforts come to fruition. Please be sure to fill in all the blanks in advance of your going to the courthouse. Please be sure you have read your testimony in advance. Once in front of the judge, please be sure to speak loud and clear.

INSTRUCTIONS FOR A DIVORCE WITH NO CHILDREN

** <u>Most courts do not allow handwritten forms and prefer typed forms</u>!!
Please check with the court before filing these papers.

Please note that "page numbers" referred to herein are the small numbers located at the upper left corner of each page.

How to fill in the "Original Petition for Divorce" form:

Page 1 - where it says "Cause Number"and "Judicial District"- leave these blank
- on the line directly under the word "OF"- Your full legal name in all capital letters
- on the line just before "COUNTY, TEXAS"- County of your residence in all capital letters
- on the line just under the word "AND"- Full legal name of your spouse in all capital letters
- paragraph A, line 1- Your full legal name
- paragraph A, line 2, 1st space- Your age
- paragraph A, line 2, 2nd space- Your county of residence
- paragraph A, line 3, 1st space- Your spouse's full legal name
- paragraph A, line 3, 2nd space- Your spouse's age
- paragraph A, line 4, 1st space- Your spouse's county of residence
- paragraph A, line 4, 2nd space- Your spouse's state of residence
- paragraph B, line 1- The name of the spouse who has lived in Texas for the last 6 months and in the Texas county for the last 90 days where the divorce is going to be filed
- paragraph D, line 1- Date of your marriage
- paragraph D, line 2- Date of your separation from your spouse

<u>USE PAGE 2 IF THE WIFE IS GOING TO CHANGE HER NAME AND DISCARD PAGE 3.</u>

Page 2 - paragraph I, line 1 - The wife's present full legal name
- paragraph I, line 2 - The name the wife wants to have

- paragraph K- The wife's present name
- on the line directly above the words "PRO SE"- Sign your name
- on the 4 lines directly under the words "PRO SE"- Print your name, your street address, City, State, Zip Code, and Telephone Number

<u>USE PAGE 3 IF THE WIFE IS NOT GOING TO CHANGE HER NAME AND DISCARD PAGE 2.</u>

Page 3 - on the line directly above the words "PRO SE"- Sign your name
- on the 4 lines directly under the words "PRO SE"- Print your name, your street address, City, State, Zip Code, and Telephone Number

How to fill in the "Waiver of Citation" form:

- Fill in the top of the form just as you did for the "Original Petition for Divorce" form except write in the number that the Clerk of the Court assigned to your case on the line after the words "Cause No."

<u>USE PAGE 1 IF HUSBAND FILES AND WIFE WANTS TO CHANGE HER NAME. DISCARD PAGE 2.</u>

Page 1 - On the line after the words "COUNTY OF", your county of residence
- paragraph A- The wife's full name
- paragraph B, line 1- The wife's full name
- paragraph B, line 2- The wife's complete street address
- paragraph C- The full name the wife wants to have

<u>USE PAGE 2 IF HUSBAND FILES AND WIFE DOES NOT WANT TO CHANGE HER NAME or IF WIFE FILES. DISCARD PAGE 1.</u>

Page 2 - On the line after the words "COUNTY OF", your county of residence
- paragraph A- Respondent's full name
- paragraph B, line 1- Respondent's full name
- paragraph B, line 2- Respondent's complete address

How to fill in the "Final Decree of Divorce" form:

- Fill in the top of the form just as you did for the "Original Petition for Divorce" form except write in the number that the Clerk of the Court assigned to your case on the line after the words "Cause No."

Page 1 - paragraph A, line 1, 1st space- Your full name
- paragraph A, line1, 2nd space- Your social security number
- paragraph A, line 2, 1st space- Your driver's license number
- paragraph A, line 2, 2nd space- Name of the State that issued your driver's license
- paragraph A, line 3, 1st space- Your spouse's full name
- paragraph A, line 3, 2nd space- Your spouse's social security number
- paragraph A, line 4, 1st space- Your spouse's driver's license number
- paragraph A, line 4, 2nd space- Name of the State that issued your spouse's driver's license
- paragraph C, second paragraph, line 1- The name of the spouse who has lived in Texas for the last 6 months and in the Texas county for the last 90 days where the divorce is filed

Page 2 - paragraph F, line 1- Your full name
- paragraph F, line 2- Your spouse's full name
- paragraph I, #6- Type in all other items of personal property that you want that you do not have in your possession. Be sure to describe the property so it can be identified easily. If you have nothing to put in this space, type in the words "no other property". Also type in the legal description of the real estate that you are going to get, if any

Page 3 - paragraph J, #6- Type in all other items of personal property that your spouse wants that he or she does not have in his or her possession. Be sure to describe the property so it can be identified easily. If nothing goes in this space, type in the words "no other property". Also type in the legal description of the real estate that Respondent is going to get, if any
- paragraph K, #2- Type in all the debts that you are going to pay. Be sure to include the name of the creditor, the account number and the total balance due

- paragraph L, #2- Type in all the debts that your spouse is going to pay. Be sure to include the name of the creditor, the account number and the total balance due

USE PAGE 4 IF THE WIFE IS NOT CHANGING HER NAME. DISCARD PAGE 5.

Page 4 - The Judge will fill in the date "SIGNED"
- On the line above the word "Petitioner", you sign
- On the line above the word "Respondent", your spouse signs

USE PAGE 5 IF THE WIFE IS CHANGING HER NAME. DISCARD PAGE 4.

Page 5 - paragraph O, line 1- The wife's current name
- paragraph O, line 2- The name the wife wants to have
- The Judge will fill in the date "SIGNED"
- On the line above the word "Petitioner", you sign
- On the line above the word "Respondent", your spouse signs

WHAT DO I DO WITH THE FORMS NOW?

1.   The first thing you should do is to put the page numbers at the bottom left of each form you just filled out. First take the "Original Petition for Divorce" and number the pages in order "1" & "2". The "Waiver of Citation" does not require any page numbers. Now take the "Final Decree of Divorce" and number the pages in order "1" through "4".

2.   Make two (2) copies of the Original Petition for Divorce and three (3) copies of the Final Decree of Divorce.

3.   Take all of your filled-out forms to the District Clerk's Office in your county, together with the exact amount of cash or a money order to pay the filing fees. The filing fees change periodically so it will be necessary for you to call the District Clerk's office and ask how much it costs to file for a divorce with no children and no service of citation. Hand the Clerk your original and both copies of the Original Petition for Divorce. The Clerk will give you back two copies with your receipt. At the top of one of the Original Petition for Divorce copies the Clerk will have written a number and assigned you to a Court.

4.   Write the Cause Number assigned to you and the Court Number on the two copies of the Original Petition for Divorce, the original and the three copies of the Agreed Decree of Divorce, and the Waiver of Citation. Give your spouse one of the Original Petitions for Divorce to keep. He or she does not have to sign this copy. Also give your spouse the **original** Waiver of Citation and all four Final Decrees of Divorce for his or her signature. Be sure to stress to your spouse that the Waiver of Citation must be signed in front of a Notary Public. Be sure you get back the **original** and all three copies of the Agreed Decree of Divorce along with the **original** Waiver of Citation. The Waiver of Citation and all four of the Final Decrees of Divorce must be signed by your spouse.

5.   Texas has a 60 day waiting period between the time you file your Original Petition for Divorce and the date you can see the Judge to get divorced. Therefore, 61 days or later from the date you completed step 2 above, you will be able to complete your divorce. On the day before you wish to finalize your divorce, call the District Clerk's office to verify

the Judge will be in and available to hear your case. Also ask the clerk what time you should be there.

6.   Before you go to court to complete your divorce, fill in your testimony on the form below. This is what you will read to the Judge in order to get your divorce. We suggest you practice reading it before your actual court date.

7.   At that predetermined time on the weekday you wish to finalize your divorce, go to the Courthouse and tell the District Clerk that you are there to finish your divorce and that you need to file-mark the Waiver of Citation and get your file. The Clerk will take your Waiver of Citation and the original of your Final Decree of Divorce. The Clerk will also have you fill out any county or state forms that are needed or required. He or she will then take you to the courtroom. Keep your copies of all other forms with you and do not present them to the Judge.

8.   Be seated until your name is called by the Judge. When your name is called, walk to the Judge's bench. The Judge will ask you to raise your right hand while he or she places you under oath. Read your courtroom testimony to the Judge as you have it filled out beginning on the next page.

Courtroom Testimony

FILL IN THE FOLLOWING BLANKS **BEFORE** YOU GO TO COURT:

Read the following to the Judge and have a copy of the Original Petition with you for any questions:

1. My name is _____.

2. I am the Petitioner in this case.

3. Immediately preceding the filing of my Petition for Divorce, _____ had lived in the State of Texas for at least 6 months and in _____ County for at least 90 days.

4. _____, who is the Respondent in this case, and I married on _____, and separated as husband and wife on _____.

5. Our marriage has become insupportable due to a discord or conflict of personalities between Respondent and myself that have destroyed the legitimate ends of our marriage.

6. There is no chance of reconciling our differences and saving our marriage.

7. There are no children born or adopted of this marriage subject to the jurisdiction of the court and none is expected.

8. Respondent has signed a Waiver of Citation and I can identify that signature.

9. Respondent and I have both signed the Final Decree of Divorce and I can identify Respondent's signature on it.

10.   I have all of the property I wish to keep in my possession at this time. Respondent has all of the property Respondent wishes to keep in his/her possession at this time.

(Read this #11 <u>only</u> if the wife wants a name change)

11.   **I would like to change my name to** _____.

                                                       OR

         My wife would like to change her name to _____.

12.   I believe this divorce decree is fair, just and equitable for both my spouse and myself.

13.   I am asking this Court to approve this Final Decree of Divorce and grant the divorce.

****

The Judge will either hand your court file to you or to the Bailiff. Either way you will be taken back to the Clerk's office by the Clerk of the Court and he or she will certify your Final Decree of Divorce copies as being correct copies of the original and hand one back to you. The Clerk will keep the other certified copy of the Final Decree of Divorce and mail it to your ex-spouse.

5

Forms:
The Divorce with No Children

This chapter contains the forms for a divorce without any children of this marriage or if you have children of this marriage who are over the age of 18 years and out of high school, or are otherwise emancipated. If you had any children born to or adopted by you during this marriage who are under the age of 18 years, are still in high school, and have not otherwise been emancipated, please go to Chapter 6 for appropriate instructions and Chapter 7 for the appropriate forms.

The Original Petition for Divorce

Pages 31, 32 and 33 of this chapter are devoted to Original Petition for Divorce. Please follow the instructions in Chapter 4 very carefully and be sure to double check your work. Correct spelling of the names is mandatory.

The Waiver of Citation

The two pages that follow the Original Petition for Divorce consist of two different Waivers of Citation. Please follow the instructions in Chapter 4 very carefully and be sure to double check your work. Correct spelling of the names is mandatory.

The Final Decree of Divorce

The last five pages of this chapter consist of your Final Decree of Divorce. Please follow the instructions in Chapter 4 very carefully and be sure to double check your work. Correct spelling of the names is mandatory as is the description of property and identification of various accounts.

CAUSE NO. _____

IN THE MATTER OF THE MARRIAGE	X	IN THE DISTRICT COURT OF
OF	X	
_____	X	_____ COUNTY, TEXAS
AND	X	
_____	X	_____ JUDICIAL DISTRICT

ORIGINAL PETITION FOR DIVORCE

A.   This divorce suit is brought by _____, hereinafter referred to as Petitioner, who is _____ years of age and who resides in _____ County, Texas.

_____, hereinafter referred to as "Respondent", is _____years of age, and resides in _____ County,_____.

B.   _____ has been a domiciliary of this state for the preceding six-month period and a resident of this county for 90 days immediately preceding the filing of this petition.

C.   No service is necessary.

D.   Petitioner and Respondent were married on _____, and ceased to live together as husband and wife on _____.

E.   The marriage of Petitioner and Respondent has become insupportable because of discord or conflict of personalities that destroys the legitimate ends of the marriage relationship and prevents any reasonable expectation of reconciliation.

F.   There are no children who were born or adopted of this marriage who are subject to the jurisdiction of this court and none is expected.

G.   Petitioner believes the parties will reach an agreement for the division of their property. If such an agreement is reached, Petitioner requests the Court to approve that agreement and order a division of their estate pursuant to that agreement.

H.   There is no protective order under any chapter or section of the Texas Family Code in effect and no application for a protective order is pending with regard to the parties to the suit.

STATEMENT CONCERNING ALTERNATIVE DISPUTE RESOLUTION

I AM AWARE THAT IT IS THE POLICY OF THE STATE OF TEXAS TO PROMOTE

THE AMICABLE AND NONJUDICIAL SETTLEMENT OF DISPUTES INVOLVING CHILDREN AND FAMILIES. I AM AWARE OF ALTERNATIVE DISPUTE RESOLUTION METHODS INCLUDING MEDIATION. WHILE I RECOGNIZE THAT ALTERNATIVE DISPUTE RESOLUTION IS AN ALTERNATIVE TO AND NOT A SUBSTITUTE FOR A TRIAL AND THAT THIS CASE MAY BE TRIED IF IT IS NOT SETTLED, I REPRESENT TO THE COURT THAT I WILL ATTEMPT IN GOOD FAITH TO RESOLVE CONTESTED ISSUES IN THIS CASE BY ALTERNATIVE DISPUTE RESOLUTION WITHOUT THE NECESSITY OF COURT INTERVENTION.

I. Petitioner requests a change of _____'s name to _____.

PRAYER

J. Petitioner prays that citation and notice issue as required by law and that the Court grant a divorce and such other relief requested in this petition.

K. Petitioner prays for a change of _____'s name.

L. Petitioner prays for general relief.

Respectfully submitted,

_____

PRO SE

_____

_____

_____

_____

THE AMICABLE AND NONJUDICIAL SETTLEMENT OF DISPUTES INVOLVING CHILDREN AND FAMILIES. I AM AWARE OF ALTERNATIVE DISPUTE RESOLUTION METHODS INCLUDING MEDIATION. WHILE I RECOGNIZE THAT ALTERNATIVE DISPUTE RESOLUTION IS AN ALTERNATIVE TO AND NOT A SUBSTITUTE FOR A TRIAL AND THAT THIS CASE MAY BE TRIED IF IT IS NOT SETTLED, I REPRESENT TO THE COURT THAT I WILL ATTEMPT IN GOOD FAITH TO RESOLVE CONTESTED ISSUES IN THIS CASE BY ALTERNATIVE DISPUTE RESOLUTION WITHOUT THE NECESSITY OF COURT INTERVENTION.

PRAYER

I.   Petitioner prays that citation and notice issue as required by law and that the Court grant a divorce and such other relief requested in this petition.

J.   Petitioner prays for general relief.

Respectfully submitted,

_____

PRO SE

_____

_____

_____

_____

1.

CAUSE NO. _____

IN THE MATTER OF THE MARRIAGE	X	IN THE DISTRICT COURT OF
OF	X	
	X	
_____	X	_____COUNTY, TEXAS
AND	X	
_____	X	_____ JUDICIAL DISTRICT

WAIVER OF CITATION

THE STATE OF TEXAS	X
COUNTY OF _____	X

A.   BEFORE ME, the undersigned authority, appeared _____,

in person, who, after being duly sworn, swore the following statements were true:

B.   "My name is _____. I am the Respondent in the above-entitled and -numbered cause. I live at _____. I have received a true copy of the Original Petition For Divorce that has been filed in this divorce case. I have read it and understand it. I enter my appearance in this divorce case for all purposes. I also waive the issuance and service of process. I agree that this divorce case may be heard and considered by the Court without any further notice to me. I also waive the making of a record of testimony in this cause."

"I further agree that the cause may be heard by the presiding Judge of the Court or by a duly appointed master of the Court."

C.   "I also request that my name be changed to _____.

_____
Respondent

SUBSCRIBED AND SWORN TO BEFORE me this _____ day of _____, _____.

I, the notary public whose signature appears below, certify that I am not an attorney for this case.

_____
Notary Public

2.

CAUSE NO. _____

IN THE MATTER OF THE MARRIAGE	X	IN THE DISTRICT COURT OF
OF	X	
_____	X	_____COUNTY, TEXAS
AND	X	
_____	X	_____ JUDICIAL DISTRICT

<u>WAIVER OF CITATION</u>

THE STATE OF TEXAS   X

COUNTY OF _____   X

A.   BEFORE ME, the undersigned authority, appeared _____,

in person, who, after being duly sworn, swore the following statements were true:

B.   "My name is _____. I am the Respondent in the above-entitled and -numbered cause. I live at _____.
I have received a true copy of the Original Petition For Divorce that has been filed in this divorce case. I have read it and understand it. I enter my appearance in this divorce case for all purposes. I also waive the issuance and service of process. I agree that this divorce case may be heard and considered by the Court without any further notice to me. I also waive the making of a record of testimony in this cause."

     "I further agree that the cause may be heard by the presiding Judge of the Court or by a duly appointed master of the Court."

_____
Respondent

SUBSCRIBED AND SWORN TO BEFORE me this ____ day of _____, _____.

I, the notary public whose signature appears below, certify that I am not an attorney for this case.

_____
Notary Public

35

CAUSE NO. _____

IN THE MATTER OF THE MARRIAGE	X	IN THE DISTRICT COURT OF
OF	X	
_____	X	_____COUNTY, TEXAS
	X	
AND	X	
_____	X	_____ JUDICIAL DISTRICT

FINAL DECREE OF DIVORCE

On this day this case came on for hearing.

A. Appearances

Petitioner, _____, Social Security number _____, driver's license number _____, _____, appeared in person, Pro Se.

Respondent, _____, Social Security number _____, driver's license number _____, _____, waived issuance and service of citation by waiver duly filed and approved this decree by signing it.

B. Record

The making of a record of testimony was waived by the parties with the consent of the Court.

C. Jurisdiction and Domicile

The Court finds that the Petitioner's pleadings are in due form and contain all the allegations, information, and prerequisites required by law. The Court finds that it has jurisdiction over this cause and the parties and that at least 60 days have elapsed since the date the suit was filed.

The Court finds _____ has been a domiciliary of this state for at least six-months immediately preceding the filing of the petition and a resident of the county in which this suit is filed for at least 90 days immediately preceding the filing of this action. All persons entitled to citation were properly cited.

D. Jury

A jury was waived, and all questions of fact and law were submitted to the Court.

E. Agreement of the Parties

The parties have agreed to the terms of this decree and further stipulate that the provisions for

Final Decree of Divorce, Page _____.

2.

division of assets and liabilities are contractual.

F.   Divorce

        IT IS ORDERED AND DECREED that _____,
Petitioner, and _____, Respondent, are divorced and that
the marriage between them is dissolved.

G.   Children of the Marriage

        The Court finds that there are no children of the marriage subject to the jurisdiction of the court
and that none is expected.

H.   Division of Marital Estate

        The parties have agreed and the Court therefore finds that the following division of the parties'
marital estate is just and right.

I.   IT IS THEREFORE ORDERED AND DECREED that Petitioner is awarded as Petitioner's sole
property the following:

        1.   All personal property and effects that are currently in the possession of Petitioner or
subject to Petitioner's sole control, unless express provision is made in this decree to the contrary.

        2.   Any and all stocks, bonds, and securities registered in Petitioner's name.

        3.   Any and all money on account in any financial institution in Petitioner's name.

        4.   All sums and proceeds from and to any and all employee benefit programs, retirement
plans and any other plans existing because of Petitioner's past, present, or future employment unless
express provision is made in this decree to the contrary.

        5.   All policies of life insurance with cash values insuring the Petitioner's life.

        6.

        IT IS FURTHER ORDERED AND DECREED that Respondent is divested of all claims and
interest in and right and title to the above property awarded to Petitioner.

J.   IT IS FURTHER ORDERED AND DECREED that Respondent is awarded as Respondent's sole
property the following:

        1.   All personal property and effects that are currently in the possession of Respondent or

3.

subject to Respondent's sole control, unless express provision is made in this decree to the contrary.

2.   Any and all stocks, bonds, and securities registered in Respondent's name.

3.   Any and all money on account in any financial institution in Respondent's name.

4.   All sums and proceeds from and to any and all employee benefit programs, retirement plans and any other plans existing because of Respondent's past, present, or future employment unless express provision is made in this decree to the contrary.

5.   All policies of life insurance, with cash values, insuring the Respondent's life.

6.

IT IS FURTHER ORDERED AND DECREED that Petitioner is divested of all claims and interest in and right and title to the above property awarded to Respondent.

K.   Petitioner IS ORDERED AND DECREED to pay the following debts and shall indemnify and hold Respondent and Respondent's property harmless from any failure to pay these debts:

1.   All debts and other obligations incurred in Petitioner's name or solely by Petitioner after the parties' date of separation unless express provision is made in this decree to the contrary.

2.

L.   Respondent IS ORDERED AND DECREED to pay the following debts and shall indemnify and hold Petitioner and Petitioner's property harmless from any failure to pay these debts:

1.   All debts and other obligations incurred in Respondent's name or solely by Respondent after the parties' date of separation unless express provision is made in this decree to the contrary.

2.

M.   Court Cost.

Court costs are to be borne by the party who incurred said costs.

N.   Clarifying Orders

The right to make orders necessary to clarify and enforce this decree is expressly reserved by this court and such reservation and right does not affect the finality of this decree.

O.   Relief Not Granted

IT IS ORDERED AND DECREED that all relief requested in this cause and not expressly granted is denied.

Date of Judgement

SIGNED on _____, _____.

_____
JUDGE PRESIDING

APPROVED AND CONSENTED TO:

_____   _____
Petitioner   Respondent

M.   <u>Court Cost.</u>

Court costs are to be borne by the party who incurred said costs.

N.   <u>Clarifying Orders</u>

The right to make orders necessary to clarify and enforce this decree is expressly reserved by this court and such reservation and right does not affect the finality of this decree.

O.   <u>Change of Name</u>

IT IS ORDERED AND DECREED that _____'s name is hereby changed to _____.

P.   <u>Relief Not Granted</u>

IT IS ORDERED AND DECREED that all relief requested in this cause and not expressly granted is denied.

<u>Date of Judgement</u>

SIGNED on _____, _____.

_____
JUDGE PRESIDING

APPROVED AND CONSENTED TO:

_____   _____
Petitioner   Respondent

6

The Divorce with Children

This chapter covers instructions for filling out the forms for a divorce with children of this marriage who are under the age of 18 years, are still in high school, and have not otherwise been emancipated. If you did not have any children born to or adopted by you during this marriage, or if all of your children of this marriage are over the age of 18 years and out of high school, or are otherwise emancipated, please go to Chapter 4 for appropriate instructions and Chapter 5 for the appropriate forms.

The Instructions

Seven pages of this chapter are devoted to instructions for filling out the Original Petition for Divorce, Waiver of Citation, the Employer's Order to Withhold Earnings for Child Support, and the Final Decree of Divorce. Please follow them very carefully and be sure to double check your work. Correct spelling of the names is mandatory as is the description of property and identification of various accounts.

What Do I Do With These Forms Now?

The four pages that follow the instructions walk you through the procedure of copying and filing with the court clerk. Pay special attention to the order of the procedure and be sure you follow it very carefully. The Original Petition for Divorce **must** be filed with the clerk's office **before** you have your spouse sign the Waiver of Citation. Any other sequence will render the Waiver of Citation void forcing you to have it signed a second time by your spouse.

The Courtroom Testimony

The last three pages of this chapter consist of your courtroom testimony. These are the "magic words" that make all your efforts come to fruition. Please be sure to fill in all the blanks in advance of your going to the courthouse. Please be sure you have read your testimony in advance. Once in front of the judge, please be sure to speak loud and clear.

INSTRUCTIONS FOR OBTAINING A DIVORCE WITH CHILDREN

Most courts do not allow handwritten forms and prefer typed forms!! Please check with the court before filling out these papers.**

Please note that "page numbers" referred to herein are the small numbers located at the upper left corner of each page.

How to fill in the "Original Petition for Divorce" form:

Page 1 - where it says "Cause Number"- leave this blank
- on the line directly under the word "OF"- Type your full legal name in all capital letters
- on the line just under the word "AND"- Type in the full legal name of your spouse in all capital letters
- on the line(s) just below the words "AND IN THE INTEREST OF", type in the full names of your child(ren) in all capital letters
- on the line just before "COUNTY, TEXAS"- Type in the county of your residence in all capital letters
- paragraph A, line 1- Your full legal name
- paragraph A, line 2, 1st space- Your age
- paragraph A, line 2, 2nd space- Your county of residence
- paragraph A, line 4- Your spouse's full legal name
- paragraph A, line 5, 1st space- Your spouse's age
- paragraph A, line 5, 2nd space- Your spouse's county of residence
- paragraph A, line 5, 3rd space- Your spouse's state of residence
- paragraph B, line 1- The name of the spouse who has lived in Texas for the last 6 months and in the Texas county for the last 90 days where the divorce is going to be filed
- paragraph D, line 1- Date of your marriage
- paragraph D, line 2- Date of your separation from your spouse

Page 2 - paragraph F- There are enough spaces for five children. Please type in the appropriate information for each of your children. On the line after "PRESENT RESIDENCE", you can just put the words "With Petitioner" if the children currently live with you, or the words "With Respondent" if the children currently live with your spouse

USE PAGE 3 IF THE WIFE IS GOING TO CHANGE HER NAME AND DISCARD PAGE 4.

Page 3 - paragraph G- Type in the name of the spouse who is going to pay child support
    - paragraph I, line 1- The wife's present full legal name
    - paragraph I, line 2- The name the wife wants to have
    - paragraph K, line 3 - The wife's present name
    - on the line directly above the words "PRO SE"- Sign your name
    - on the 4 lines directly under the words "PRO SE"- Type in your name, street address, City, State, Zip Code, and Telephone Number

USE PAGE 4 IF THE WIFE IS NOT GOING TO CHANGE HER NAME AND DISCARD PAGE 3.

Page 4 - paragraph G- Type in the name of the spouse who is going to pay child support
    - on the line directly above the words "PRO SE"- Sign your name
    - on the 4 lines directly under the words "PRO SE"- Type in your name, street address, City, State, Zip Code, and Telephone Number

How to fill out the "Waiver of Citation" form:

    - Fill in the top of the form just as you did for the "Original Petition for Divorce" form except write in the number that the Clerk of the Court assigned to your case on the line after the words "Cause No."

USE PAGES 1 & 2 IF HUSBAND FILES AND WIFE DOES NOT WANT TO CHANGE HER NAME or IF WIFE FILES. DISCARD PAGES 3 & 4.

Page 1 - On the line after the words "COUNTY OF", type in your county of residence
    - paragraph A- Respondent's full name

- paragraph B, line 1- Respondent's full name

- paragraph B, line 2- Respondent's complete street address

USE PAGES 3 & 4 IF HUSBAND FILES AND WIFE DOES WANT TO CHANGE HER NAME. DISCARD PAGES 1 & 2.

Page 3 - On the line after the words "COUNTY OF", type in your county of residence

    - paragraph A- Respondent's full name

    - paragraph B, line 1- Respondent's full name

    - paragraph B, line 2- Respondent's complete address

Page 4 - paragraph C, line 1- Wife's present name

    - paragraph C, line 2- Name wife wants to have

How to fill out the "Employer's Order to Withhold Earning for Child Support":

    - Fill in the top of the form just as you did for the "Original Petition for Divorce" form except write in the number that the Clerk of the Court assigned to your case on the line after the words "Cause No."

Page 1 - paragraph A, line 1- The full name of the spouse who is going to pay child support

    - paragraph B, line 1- The full name of the spouse who is going to pay child support

    - paragraph B, line 2- The street address of the spouse who is going to pay child support

    - paragraph B, line 3- The city, state & zip code of the spouse who is going to pay child support

    - paragraph B, line 4- The social security number of the spouse who is going to pay child support

    - paragraph C, line 1- The full name of the spouse who is going to receive child support

    - paragraph C, line 2- The social security number of the spouse who is going to receive child support

Page 2 - paragraph D- There are enough spaces for five children. Please type in the appropriate information for each of your children. If a blank does not apply, such as your child has no driver's license, put "NONE" on the blank line

Page 3 - paragraph G, line 2- Name of the county where you are getting your divorce

- paragraph G, line 4- Full name of the spouse who is going to pay child support

- paragraph G, line 5- Full name of the spouse who is going to receive child support

- paragraph G, line 6- The number the Court Clerk assigned to your divorce case. It is the number that is written at the top of your "Original Petition for Divorce" on the "Cause No." line

- paragraph G, line 7- The child support account number that was assigned by your county's child support office goes here

- paragraph H, #1- The dollar amount of child support to be paid monthly

Page 4 - paragraph H, #2- The dollar amount of child support to be paid twice a month

- paragraph H, #3- The dollar amount of child support to be paid every other week, such as every other Friday

- paragraph H, #4- The dollar amount of child support to be paid every week

Page 5 - On the line after the word "SIGNED", the Judge will fill in the date.

How to fill out the "Final Decree of Divorce" form:

- Fill in the top of the form just as you did for the "Original Petition for Divorce" form except write in the number that the Clerk of the Court assigned to your case on the line after the words "Cause No."

Page 1 - paragraph A, line 1, 1st space- Your full name

- paragraph A, line 2, 1st space- Your social security number

- paragraph A, line 2, 2nd space- Your driver's license number

- paragraph A, line 3- Name of the State that issued your driver's license

- paragraph A, line 4- Your spouse's full name

- paragraph A, line 5, 1st space- Your spouse's social security number

- paragraph A, line 5, 2nd space- Your spouse's driver's license number

- paragraph A, line 6- Name of the State that issued your spouse's driver's license

Page 2 - paragraph F, line 1- Your full name

- paragraph F, line 2- Your spouse's full name

- paragraph G- There are enough spaces for five children. Please type in the appropriate information for each of your children. On the line after "PRESENT RESIDENCE", you can just put the words "With Petitioner" if the children currently live with you, or the words "With Respondent" if the children currently live with your spouse

Page 3 - paragraph I, line 3-The full name of the spouse with whom the child will live on a permanent basis
- paragraph I, line 5- The full name of the spouse who will have visitation with the children and who will pay child support

Page 11- paragraph L, line1- The full name of the spouse who is going to pay child support
- paragraph L, line 4, 1st space- The full name of the spouse who is going to receive child support
- paragraph L, line 4, 2nd space- The dollar amount of child support to be paid figured on a monthly basis (see page 23, #7, for instructions on how to calculate the amount of child support to be paid)
- paragraph L, line 5- Type in the first date that the child support will be paid, such as November 13, 2001)

Page 12- paragraph M, line 13, 1st space- The dollar amount of child support to be paid monthly
- paragraph M, line 13, 2nd space- The dollar amount of child support to be paid twice a month
- paragraph M, line 13, 3rd space- The dollar amount of child support to be paid every other week, such as every other Friday
- paragraph M, line 13, 4th space- The dollar amount of child support to be paid every week

Page 13 - paragraph N, line 2- The name of your county of residence (the county you filed your divorce in)
- paragraph N, line 3- The full name of the spouse who is going to receive the child support payments
- paragraph O, line 2, 1st space- The name of your county of residence
- paragraph O, line 2, 2nd space- The dollar amount that your county's child support office is going to charge you and your spouse on a yearly basis to keep the child

support payment records. You get this figure from your county's child support office

 - paragraph O, line 3- The dollar amount that will be due on the day you get your divorce. You get this figure from your county's child support office

 - paragraph O, line 4, 1st space- The date you get your divorce

 - paragraph O, line 4, 2nd space- The dollar amount that your county's child support office is going to charge you and your spouse on a yearly basis to keep the child support payment records. You get this figure from your county's child support office

 - paragraph O, line 5, 1st space- The day you get your divorce (such as the 21st)

 - paragraph O, line 5, 2nd space- The month you get your divorce (such as July)

 - paragraph P- The full name of the spouse who is going to receive the child support

Page 14- paragraph Q, 1., line 1- The full name of the spouse who is going to be responsible for paying for the health insurance for the child(ren)

 - paragraph Q, 1., line 4 - The full name of the spouse who is not going to be responsible for paying for the health insurance for the child(ren)

Page 18- paragraph S, 6. - Type in all other items of personal property that you want that you do not have in your possession. Be sure to describe the property so it can be identified easily. If you have nothing to put in this space, type in the words "no other property". Also type in the legal description of the real estate that you are going to get , if any

 - paragraph T, 6. - Type in all other items of personal property that your spouse wants that he or she does not have in his or her possession. Be sure to describe the property so it can be identified easily. If nothing goes in this space, type in the words "no other property". Also type in the legal description of the real estate that you are going to get , if any

Page 19- paragraph U, #2- Type in all the debts that you are going to pay. Be sure to include the name of the creditor, the account number and the total balance due

 - paragraph V, #2- Type in all the debts that your spouse is going to pay. Be sure to include the name of the creditor, the account number and the total balance due

<u>USE PAGE 20 IF THE WIFE IS CHANGING HER NAME. DISCARD PAGE 21</u>.

Page 20- paragraph Y, line 1- The full name of the wife

      - paragraph Y, line 2- The full name the wife wants to have

      - The Judge will fill in the date "SIGNED"

      - On the line above the word "Petitioner", you sign.

      - On the line above the word "Respondent", your spouse signs.

<u>USE PAGE 21 IF THE WIFE IS NOT CHANGING HER NAME. DISCARD PAGE 20</u>.

Page 20- The Judge will fill in the date "SIGNED"

      - On the line above the word "Petitioner", you sign

      - On the line above the word "Respondent", your spouse signs

WHAT DO I DO WITH THE FORMS NOW?

1. The first thing you should do is to put the page numbers at the bottom left of each form you just filled out. First take the "Original Petition for Divorce" and number the pages in order "1, 2 & 3". The "Waiver of Citation" needs to be numbered pages "1 & 2". The "Employer's Order to Withhold Earnings for Child Support" does not require any page numbers. The "Final Decree of Divorce" needs to be numbered pages "1" through "19".

2. Make two (2) copies of the ORIGINAL PETITION FOR DIVORCE and five (5) copies of the FINAL DECREE OF DIVORCE and five (5) copies of the EMPLOYER'S ORDER TO WITHHOLD EARNINGS FOR CHILD SUPPORT.

3. The filing fees change periodically so it will be necessary for you to call the District Clerk's office in your county and ask how much it costs to file for a divorce **with children and no service of citation**. When you are ready to file your divorce, take <u>all</u> of your filled-out forms to the District Clerk's Office, together with the exact amount of **cash or a money order** to pay the filing fees. Hand the Clerk your original and both copies of the Original Petition for Divorce. The Clerk will return two copies to you with your receipt. At the top of one of the Original Petition for Divorce copies the Clerk will have written a number and assigned you to a Court. **Ask the Clerk** to give you all of the court forms so you can fill them out. (You will be able to take these forms with you to fill out. The Court will not need them until your scheduled date to finalize.)

4. Write the Cause Number assigned to you and the Court Number on the two copies of the Original Petition for Divorce, the original <u>and</u> the five copies of the Final Decree of Divorce, the Waiver of Citation, and the original <u>and</u> the five copies of the Employer's Order to Withhold Earnings for Child Support. Each document and each copy must have your Cause Number and Court Number written on it. You may also sign the **original** Final Decree of Divorce and all of the copies where your signature blank is located.

5. Now it is time to calculate the amount of child support under Texas law that must be paid to the party who will have the child(ren) live with him or her. DO ALL CALCULATIONS BASED ON MONTHLY INCOME.

First you determine the disposable earnings of the person who will not have the child(ren) living with him or her that are subject to withholding for child support. To do this you add up all of the non-custodial parent's earnings, including all wages, salaries, overtime pay, severance pay, commissions, bonuses, tips, retirement benefits, pensions, annuities, workers compensation benefits, disability benefits and unemployment benefits.

Then you deduct the following to determine disposable earnings from which child support will be calculated: Federal Income Tax based on the tax rate for a single person claiming 1 personal exemption and the standard deduction, Social Security Tax, Union Dues, Retirement Contributions if they are mandatory contributions only, Cost of Health and Dental Insurance for the children only, Railroad Retirement Act Contributions, and State Income Tax (if any).

Next you take this disposable earnings amount for the month and multiply it by 20% for 1 child, 25% for 2 children, 30% for 3 children, 35% for 4 children, and 40% for 5 children. This gives you the amount of monthly child support that must be paid under Texas law. Fill in the appropriate amounts in the "Final Decree of Divorce" and the "Employer's Order to Withhold Earnings for Child Support."

6.   At this point you are ready to give your spouse the following: one of the copies of the Original Petitions for Divorce to keep, the **original** Waiver of Citation to sign and have notarized, **and** the **original** Final Decree of Divorce with the five copies for your spouse's signature. Be sure to stress to your spouse that the Waiver of Citation <u>must</u> be signed in front of a Notary Public. It is not valid unless it is signed correctly. (NOTE: The Final Decree must be signed by both of you, but does not require notarization for either party - only the WAIVER OF CITATION requires notarization) Be <u>sure</u> you get back the **original** <u>and</u> all five copies of the Final Decree of Divorce along with the **original** Waiver of Citation from your spouse.

7.   Also fill out each form that the Clerk gave you. You will need to take all of these forms with you later, when you go to Court to finalize your divorce. (You will not have time in Court to fill them out)

8.   Texas has a 60 day waiting period between the time you file your Original Petition for Divorce and the date you can see the Judge to finalize your divorce. Therefore, 61 days or

later from the date you completed step 2 above, you will be able to complete your divorce. (NOTE: If you forget what date you filed your divorce on, check the file-mark stamped date on your ORIGINAL PETITION FOR DIVORCE copy) About one week before you wish to finalize your divorce, call the District Clerk to verify that the Judge will be in and available to hear your case. (In some courts, you must schedule a specific date and time to finalize)

NOTE: It is highly recommended that you practice reading your Court Testimony before you appear in Court. You want to be completely prepared to finalize your divorce in an efficient manner. You will need to dress with respect for the Judge. Most courts do not allow jeans, t-shirts, or shorts. Ask the Court Clerk, ahead of time, if you have any questions concerning dress.

9. Only the Petitioner (the person that **filed** the divorce) appears in Court to finalize. The Respondent (the person that signed the Waiver) does not go to Court to finalize. The Respondent will be mailed a certified copy of the Final Decree of Divorce and the Employer's Order to Withhold Earnings for Child Support from the Clerk's office when the divorce has been finalized.

10. On the day you are going to finalize your divorce, arrive at the courthouse about one-half hour before the time your divorce is scheduled to be heard by the Judge. (**VERY IMPORTANT NOTE:** Make sure that you have with you the following documents: one WAIVER OF CITATION that has been signed by your spouse and notarized, one copy of the ORIGINAL PETITION FOR DIVORCE, one original FINAL DECREE OF DIVORCE with the five copies, one original EMPLOYER'S ORDER TO WITHHOLD EARNINGS FOR CHILD SUPPORT with the five copies, the completed forms you got from the clerk, these instructions, and YOUR COURT TESTIMONY with all blanks filled in) Go to the District Clerk's Office, and tell the Clerk that you are there to finalize your divorce **and** you need to **file-mark** the Waiver of Citation. The Clerk will assist you or direct you to the proper party who will then take your Waiver of Citation, the other forms the clerk gave you earlier, the original of your Final Decree of Divorce and the original of your Employer's Order to Withhold Earnings for Child Support. He or she will then make sure that both you and your file get to the proper courtroom. Keep your copies of all other forms with you and do not present them to the Judge.

11. Be seated until your name is called by the Judge. (Make sure you have a copy of the Original Petition in front of you and that your testimony is ready to read to the Judge) When your name is called, walk to the Judge's bench. The Judge will ask you to raise your right hand while you are sworn in. Read your courtroom testimony to the Judge as you have it filled out beginning on the next page.

Courtroom Testimony

<u>FILL IN THE FOLLOWING BLANKS **BEFORE** YOU GO TO COURT</u>

Read the following to the Judge and have a copy of the Original Petition with you for any questions.

1.   My name is _____.

2.   I am the Petitioner in this case.

3.   Immediately preceding the filing of my Petition for Divorce, _____ had lived in the State of Texas for at least 6 months and in _____ County for at least 90 days.

4.   Respondent has signed a Waiver of Citation and I can identify that signature.

5.   _____, who is the Respondent in this case, and I married on _____, and separated as husband and wife on _____.

6.   Our marriage has become insupportable due to a discord or conflict of personalities between Respondent and myself that have destroyed the legitimate ends of our marriage.

7.   There is no chance of reconciling our differences and saving our marriage.

8.   There were/was _____ child(ren) born or adopted of this marriage. No other children are expected.

9.   There are no court orders affecting the child(ren).

10.   No property is owned or possessed by the child(ren).

(Read this #11 only if you or your spouse want a name change)

11.   **I would like to change my name to _____.**
              OR
       My wife would like to change her name to _____.

12.   Respondent and I have both signed the Final Decree of Divorce and I can identify Respondent's signature on it.

13.   My spouse and I have agreed on being named Joint Managing Conservators of our child(ren), with _____ being named the Primary Joint Managing Conservator and having the sole right to establish the primary physical residence of the child(ren).

14.   _____ will have standard visitation and pay child support in the amount of $_____ per month.

15.   This amount of child support is _____% of _____'s net income.

16.   My spouse and I have agreed that the child support to be paid shall be withheld from earnings and paid through the child support office.

17.   My spouse and I have also agreed that _____ will carry health insurance on the child(ren) and each of us will pay one-half of all medical and dental bills that are not paid by insurance.

18.   I have all of the property I wish to keep in my possession at this time and Respondent has all of the property Respondent wishes to keep in Respondent's possession at this time.

19.   My spouse and I have made provisions for the division of our marital debts as set forth in the Final Decree of Divorce.

20.   I believe this divorce decree is fair, just and equitable for both my spouse and myself.

21.   I believe this divorce decree is in the best interest of my child(ren).

22.   I am asking this Court to approve this Final Decree of Divorce and grant the divorce.

****

The Judge will either hand your court file to you or to the Bailiff. Either way you will be taken back to the Clerk's office by the Clerk of the Court and he or she will certify your Final Decree of Divorce copies as being correct copies of the original and hand one back to you. The Clerk will keep the other certified copy of the Final Decree of Divorce and mail it to your ex-spouse.

7

Forms:
The Divorce with Children

This chapter contains the forms for a divorce with children of this marriage who are under the age of 18 years, are still in high school, and have not otherwise been emancipated. If you did not have any children born to or adopted by you during this marriage, or if all of your children of this marriage are over the age of 18 years and out high school, or are otherwise emancipated, please go to Chapter 4 for appropriate instructions and Chapter 5 for the appropriate forms.

The Original Petition for Divorce

Four pages of this chapter are devoted to Original Petition for Divorce. Please follow the instructions in Chapter 6 very carefully and be sure to double check your work. Correct spelling of the names is mandatory.

The Waiver of Citation

The four pages that follow the Original Petition for Divorce consist of two different Waivers of Citation. Please follow the instructions in Chapter 6 very carefully and be sure to double check your work. Correct spelling of the names is mandatory.

The Employer's Order to Withhold Earnings for Child Support

The next five pages consist of the Employer's Order to Withhold Earnings for Child Support. Please follow the instructions in Chapter 6 very carefully and be sure to double check your work. Correct spelling of the names is mandatory.

The Final Decree of Divorce

The last twenty-one pages of this chapter consist of your Final Decree of Divorce. Please follow the instructions in Chapter 6 very carefully and be sure to double check your work. Correct spelling of the names is mandatory as is the description of property and identification of various accounts.

CAUSE NO._____

IN THE MATTER OF THE MARRIAGE OF	X	IN THE DISTRICT COURT
_____	X	
AND		
_____	X	_____ JUDICIAL DISTRICT
AND IN THE INTEREST OF		
_____	X	
_____		
_____	X	
_____		
_____,		
CHILD(REN)	X	_____COUNTY, TEXAS

ORIGINAL PETITION FOR DIVORCE

A.   This divorce suit is brought by _____, hereinafter referred to as Petitioner, who is _____ years of age and who resides in _____ County, Texas.
_____, hereinafter referred to as Respondent, is _____ years of age and resides in _____ County, _____.

B.   _____ has been a domiciliary of this state for the preceding six-month period and a resident of this county for 90 days immediately preceding the filing of this petition.

C.   No service is necessary.

D.   Petitioner and Respondent were married on _____, and ceased to live together as husband and wife on _____.

E.   The marriage of Petitioner and Respondent has become insupportable because of discord or conflict of personalities that destroys the legitimate ends of the marriage relationship and prevents any reasonable expectation of reconciliation.

2.

F.   Petitioner and Respondent are parents of the following child(ren) of this marriage who are not under the continuing jurisdiction of any other court:

NAME: _____

SEX: _____   BIRTH DATE: _____

BIRTHPLACE: _____

PRESENT RESIDENCE: _____

NAME: _____

SEX: _____   BIRTH DATE: _____

BIRTHPLACE: _____

PRESENT RESIDENCE: _____

NAME: _____

SEX: _____   BIRTH DATE: _____

BIRTHPLACE: _____

PRESENT RESIDENCE: _____

NAME: _____

SEX: _____   BIRTH DATE: _____

BIRTHPLACE: _____

PRESENT RESIDENCE: _____

NAME: _____

SEX: _____   BIRTH DATE: _____

BIRTHPLACE: _____

PRESENT RESIDENCE: _____

There are no court-ordered conservatorships, court-ordered guardianships, or other court-ordered relationships affecting the child(ren). No property is owned or possessed by the child(ren).

G.   Petitioner and Respondent should be appointed joint managing conservators, with all the rights, privileges, duties, and powers of a parent conservator, and _____ should be ordered to make payments for the support of the child(ren).

H.   Petitioner believes the parties will reach an agreement for the division of their property. If such agreement is reached, Petitioner requests the Court to approve that agreement and order a division of their estate pursuant to that agreement.

I.   Petitioner requests a change of _____'s name to _____.

J.   There is no protective order under any chapter or section of the Texas Family Code in effect and no application for a protective order is pending with regard to the parties to the suit.

STATEMENT CONCERNING ALTERNATIVE DISPUTE RESOLUTION

I AM AWARE THAT IT IS THE POLICY OF THE STATE OF TEXAS TO PROMOTE THE AMICABLE AND NONJUDICIAL SETTLEMENT OF DISPUTES INVOLVING CHILDREN AND FAMILIES. I AM AWARE OF ALTERNATIVE DISPUTE RESOLUTION METHODS INCLUDING MEDIATION. WHILE I RECOGNIZE THAT ALTERNATIVE DISPUTE RESOLUTION IS AN ALTERNATIVE TO AND NOT A SUBSTITUTE FOR A TRIAL AND THAT THIS CASE MAY BE TRIED IF IT IS NOT SETTLED, I REPRESENT TO THE COURT THAT I WILL ATTEMPT IN GOOD FAITH TO RESOLVE CONTESTED ISSUES IN THIS CASE BY ALTERNATIVE DISPUTE RESOLUTION WITHOUT THE NECESSITY OF COURT INTERVENTION.

PRAYER

K.   Petitioner prays that citation and notice issue as required by law and that the Court grant a divorce and such other relief requested in this petition.

Petitioner prays for a change of _____'s name.

Petitioner prays for general relief.

PRO SE _____

_____

_____

_____

_____

There are no court-ordered conservatorships, court-ordered guardianships, or other court-ordered relationships affecting the child(ren).

No property is owned or possessed by the child(ren).

G.   Petitioner and Respondent should be appointed joint managing conservators, with all the rights, privileges, duties, and powers of a parent conservator, and _____ should be ordered to make payments for the support of the child(ren).

H.   Petitioner believes the parties will reach an agreement for the division of their property. If such agreement is reached, Petitioner requests the Court to approve that agreement and order a division of their estate pursuant to that agreement.

I.   There is no protective order under any chapter or section of the Texas Family Code in effect and no application for a protective order is pending with regard to the parties to the suit.

STATEMENT CONCERNING ALTERNATIVE DISPUTE RESOLUTION

I AM AWARE THAT IT IS THE POLICY OF THE STATE OF TEXAS TO PROMOTE THE AMICABLE AND NONJUDICIAL SETTLEMENT OF DISPUTES INVOLVING CHILDREN AND FAMILIES. I AM AWARE OF ALTERNATIVE DISPUTE RESOLUTION METHODS INCLUDING MEDIATION. WHILE I RECOGNIZE THAT ALTERNATIVE DISPUTE RESOLUTION IS AN ALTERNATIVE TO AND NOT A SUBSTITUTE FOR A TRIAL AND THAT THIS CASE MAY BE TRIED IF IT IS NOT SETTLED, I REPRESENT TO THE COURT THAT I WILL ATTEMPT IN GOOD FAITH TO RESOLVE CONTESTED ISSUES IN THIS CASE BY ALTERNATIVE DISPUTE RESOLUTION WITHOUT THE NECESSITY OF COURT INTERVENTION.

PRAYER

J.   Petitioner prays that citation and notice issue as required by law and that the Court grant a divorce and such other relief requested in this petition.

Petitioner prays for general relief.

_____
PRO SE

_____

_____

_____

_____

CAUSE NO._____

IN THE MATTER OF THE MARRIAGE   X   IN THE DISTRICT COURT
OF

_____   X

AND

_____   X   _____JUDICIAL DISTRICT

AND IN THE INTEREST OF

_____   X

_____

_____   X

_____

_____,
CHILD(REN)   X   _____COUNTY, TEXAS

WAIVER OF CITATION

THE STATE OF TEXAS   X
COUNTY OF_____   X

A.   BEFORE ME, the undersigned authority, appeared _____,
in person, who, after being duly sworn, swore the following statements made were true:

B.   "My name is _____. I am the Respondent in the above-entitled
and -numbered cause. I live at _____.
I have received a true copy of the Original Petition For Divorce that has been filed in this divorce
case. I have read it and understand it. I enter my appearance in this divorce case for all purposes. I
also waive the issuance and service of process. I agree that this divorce case may be heard and
considered by the Court without any further notice to me. I further waive the making of a record of
testimony in this cause."

2.

"I also agree that this divorce case may be heard by the presiding Judge of the Court or by a duly appointed Master or Associate Judge of the Court."

_____
Respondent

SUBSCRIBED AND SWORN TO BEFORE me this _____ day of

_____, _____.

I, the notary public whose signature appears below, certify that I am not an attorney for this

case.

_____
Notary Public

3.

CAUSE NO._____

IN THE MATTER OF THE MARRIAGE OF	X	IN THE DISTRICT COURT
_____	X	
AND		
_____	X	_____JUDICIAL DISTRICT
AND IN THE INTEREST OF		
_____	X	
_____		
_____	X	
_____		
_____,	X	_____COUNTY, TEXAS
CHILD(REN)		

WAIVER OF CITATION

THE STATE OF TEXAS   X
COUNTY OF_____   X

A.   BEFORE ME, the undersigned authority, appeared _____, in person, who, after being duly sworn, swore the following statements made were true:

B.   "My name is _____. I am the Respondent in the above-entitled and -numbered cause. I live at _____. I have received a true copy of the Original Petition For Divorce that has been filed in this divorce case. I have read it and understand it. I enter my appearance in this divorce case for all purposes. I also waive the issuance and service of process. I agree that this divorce case may be heard and considered by the Court without any further notice to me. I further waive the making of a record of testimony in this cause."

4.

C. _____ requests a name change to

_____.

       "I also agree that this divorce case may be heard by the presiding Judge of the Court or by a duly appointed Master or Associate Judge of the Court."

_____
                          Respondent

       SUBSCRIBED AND SWORN TO BEFORE me this _____ day of

_____, _____.

       I, the notary public whose signature appears below, certify that I am not an attorney for this

case.

_____
                          Notary Public

CAUSE NO._____

IN THE MATTER OF THE MARRIAGE OF	X	IN THE DISTRICT COURT
_____	X	
AND		
_____	X	_____JUDICIAL DISTRICT
AND IN THE INTEREST OF		
_____	X	
_____		
_____	X	
_____		
_____ ,		
CHILD(REN)	X	_____COUNTY, TEXAS

EMPLOYER'S ORDER TO WITHHOLD EARNINGS FOR CHILD SUPPORT

A.   The Court ORDERS you, the employer of _____ , to withhold income from the Obligor's disposable earnings from his employment with you as set below:

B.   **Obligor**

NAME: _____

ADDRESS: _____

_____

SOCIAL SECURITY NUMBER: _____

C.   **Obligee**

NAME: _____

SOCIAL SECURITY NUMBER: _____

2

D.   **Child(ren)**

NAME:_____

SEX:_____ BIRTHDATE:_____

BIRTHPLACE: _____

SOCIAL SECURITY NO:_____ DRIVER'S LICENSE NO: _____

NAME:_____

SEX:_____ BIRTHDATE:_____

BIRTHPLACE: _____

SOCIAL SECURITY NO:_____ DRIVER'S LICENSE NO: _____

NAME:_____

SEX:_____ BIRTHDATE:_____

BIRTHPLACE: _____

SOCIAL SECURITY NO:_____ DRIVER'S LICENSE NO: _____

NAME:_____

SEX:_____ BIRTHDATE:_____

BIRTHPLACE: _____

SOCIAL SECURITY NO:_____ DRIVER'S LICENSE NO: _____

NAME:_____

SEX:_____ BIRTHDATE:_____

BIRTHPLACE: _____

SOCIAL SECURITY NO:_____ DRIVER'S LICENSE NO: _____

E.   **Income Withholding Law**

Attached to this Employer's Order to Withhold Earnings for Child Support is a copy of the Texas Family Code, Chapter 158, Subchapter C. This Chapter and Subchapter set forth the rights and duties as well as the potential liabilities of employers, in addition to the provisions of this order.

F.   **Withholding of Earnings**

The Court further ORDERS that any employer of Obligor shall begin withholding from the Obligor's disposable earnings no later than the first pay period following the date this order is served on that employer.

G.   **Method of Payment**

The Court further ORDERS the employer to pay any and all amounts withheld on each pay day through the _____ County Child Support Office for distribution under the law. All payments shall be identified by:

Obligor's name:_____

Obligee's name:_____

Cause number:_____

Child Support Account Number:_____ and the date on which the withholding occurred.

H.   **Maximum Amount to be Withheld**

The maximum amount to be withheld by the Obligor's employer shall not exceed 50 percent of Obligor's disposable earnings.

This Court further ORDERS the employer of the Obligor to withhold the following amounts from the earnings of Obligor:

1. $_____ if the Obligor is PAID MONTHLY.

2. $\underline{\hspace{3cm}}$ if the Obligor is PAID TWICE MONTHLY.

3. $\underline{\hspace{3cm}}$ if the Obligor is PAID EVERY OTHER WEEK.

4. $\underline{\hspace{3cm}}$ if the Obligor is PAID EVERY WEEK.

Obligor's employer is ORDERED AND DECREED to continue to withhold the above-referenced amounts from Obligor's earnings until the first month following the date of the occurrence of one of the events set forth below.

(1)   The youngest child reaches the age of 18 years, provided that, if the child is fully enrolled in an accredited primary or secondary school in a program leading toward a high school diploma, the periodic child-support payments shall continue to be due until the first day of the first month following graduation from high school;

(2)   The youngest child marries;

(3)   The youngest child dies;

(4)   The youngest child's disabilities are otherwise removed for general purposes;

(5)   The youngest child is otherwise emancipated; or

(6)   Further order modifying this child support.

I.   **Calculating Disposable Earnings**

The Obligor's disposable earnings that are subject to withholding for child support under this order shall be calculated by the employer as follows:

A.   First determine the "earnings" of Obligor. This means all wages, salaries, or compensations received for personal services including overtime pay, severance pay, commission, bonuses, tips, retirement benefits, pensions, annuities, workers compensation benefits, disability benefits and unemployment benefits;

B.   Then deduct the following items to determine Obligor's disposable earnings:
  (a)   Federal FICA or OASI tax (Social Security), and
  (b)   union dues; and
  (c)   nondiscretionary retirement contributions by the Obligor; and
  (d)   expenses for health insurance coverage for Obligor's aforenamed children; and
  (e)   Railroad Retirement Act contributions; and
  (f)   Federal Income Tax based on the tax rate for a single person claiming one (1) personal exemption and the standard deduction; and
  (g)   State Income Tax.

J.   **Multiple Withholding Orders**

In the event that you, the Obligor's employer, receive more than one "Employer's Order to Withhold Earnings for Child Support" for the Obligor, you are ordered and therefore shall pay an equal amount towards the current support portion of all orders until each is individually complied with.

K.   **Change of Employment Notice**

The Court further ORDERS you, the employer, to notify this Court and the Obligee within seven days of Obligor's employment termination date. This Court also ORDERS you, the employer, to provide the last known address of the Obligor, and the name and address of the Obligor's new employer, if known.

Signed:_____

_____
JUDGE PRESIDING

Employer's Order to Withhold Earnings for Child Support, Page 5.

73

CAUSE NO._____

IN THE MATTER OF THE MARRIAGE OF	X	IN THE DISTRICT COURT
_____	X	
AND		
_____	X	_____JUDICIAL DISTRICT
AND IN THE INTEREST OF		
_____	X	
_____		
_____	X	
_____		
_____,	X	_____COUNTY, TEXAS
CHILD(REN)		

FINAL DECREE OF DIVORCE

On this date this case came on for hearing.

A.   Appearances.

Petitioner, _____, Social Security number _____, driver's license number _____, _____, appeared in person, Pro Se.

Respondent, _____, Social Security number _____, driver's license number _____, _____, waived issuance and service of citation and approved this decree as signing it.

B.   Record.

The making of a record of testimony was waived.

C.   Jurisdiction and Domicile.

The Court finds that the Petitioner's pleadings are in due form and contain all the allegations, information, and prerequisites required by law. The Court finds that it has jurisdiction over this cause and the parties and that at least 60 days have elapsed since the date the suit was filed. The Court finds that Petitioner has been a domiciliary of this state for at least six months immediately preceding the filing of the petition and a resident of the county in which this suit is filed for at least 90 days immediately preceding the filing of this action. All persons entitled to citation were properly cited.

D.   Jury.

A jury was waived, and all questions of fact and law were submitted to the Court.

E.   Agreement of the Parties.

The parties have agreed to the terms of this decree.

F.   Divorce.

IT IS ORDERED AND DECREED that _____, Petitioner, and _____, Respondent, are divorced and that the marriage between them is dissolved.

G.   Child(ren)of the Marriage.

The Court finds that Petitioner and Respondent are the parents of the following child(ren):

NAME: _____

SEX: _____   BIRTHPLACE: _____

BIRTH DATE: _____

PRESENT RESIDENCE: _____

NAME: _____

SEX: _____   BIRTHPLACE: _____

BIRTH DATE: _____

PRESENT RESIDENCE: _____

NAME: _____

SEX: _____ BIRTHPLACE: _____

BIRTH DATE: _____

PRESENT RESIDENCE: _____

NAME: _____

SEX: _____ BIRTHPLACE: _____

BIRTH DATE: _____

PRESENT RESIDENCE: _____

NAME: _____

SEX: _____ BIRTHPLACE: _____

BIRTH DATE: _____

PRESENT RESIDENCE: _____

H.   Conservatorship and Support.

After considering all the circumstances of the parties and of their child(ren), the Court finds the following orders are in the best interest of the child(ren):

I.   Joint Managing Conservators.

IT IS ORDERED AND DECREED that Petitioner and Respondent are appointed Joint Managing Conservators of the child(ren).

_____ is ORDERED named the Primary Joint Managing Conservator of the child(ren) and

_____ is ORDERED named the Joint Managing Conservator for purposes of the visitation schedule set forth below.

IT IS ORDERED AND DECREED that at all times Petitioner and Respondent shall each retain the right:

(a)   to receive information from the other parent concerning the health, education, and welfare of the child(ren); and

(b)   to confer with the other parent to the extent possible before making a decision concerning the health, education, and welfare of the child(ren);

(c)   of access to medical, dental, psychological and educational records of the child(ren);

(d)   to consult with a physician, dentist or psychologist of the child(ren);

(e)   to consult with school officials concerning the child(ren)'s welfare and educational status, including school activities;

(f)   to attend school activities of the child(ren);

(g)   to be designated on the child(ren)'s records as a person to be notified in case of an emergency;

(h)   to consent to medical, dental, and surgical treatment during an emergency involving an immediate danger to the health and safety of the child(ren); and

(i)   to manage the estate of the child(ren) to the extent the estates have been created by the parent or the parent's family.

IT IS ORDERED that, at all times, Petitioner and Respondent, as parent joint managing conservators, shall each have the following duties:

(a)   the duty to inform the other parent in a timely manner of significant information concerning the health, education, and welfare of the child(ren); and

(b)   the duty to inform the other parent if the parent resides with for at least 30 days, marries, or intends to marry a person who the parent knows is registered as a sex offender under Chapter 62, Code of Criminal Procedure, as added by Chapter 668, Acts of the 75th Legislature, Regular Session, 1997; or is currently charged with an offense for which on conviction the person would be required to register under that chapter. IT IS ORDERED that this information be noticed on the other parent as soon as practicable but not later than the 40th day after the date the parent begins to reside with the person or the 10th day after the date the marriage occurs, as appropriate. IT IS FURTHER ORDERED that the notice must include a description of the offense that is the basis of the person's requirement to register as a sex offender or of the offense with which the person is charged. WARNING: A PERSON COMMITS AN OFFENSE IF THE PERSON FAILS TO PROVIDE NOTICE IN THE MANNER REQUIRED ABOVE. AN OFFENSE UNDER THIS PROVISION IS A CLASS C MISDEMEANOR.

5.

IT IS ORDERED AND DECREED that Petitioner and Respondent shall each retain the following rights and duties during their respective periods of possession:

(a)   the duty of care, control, protection, and reasonable discipline of the child(ren);

(b)   the duty to support the child(ren), including providing the child(ren) with clothing, food, shelter, and medical and dental care not involving an invasive procedure;

(c)   the right to consent for the child(ren) to medical and dental care not involving an invasive procedure;

(d)   the right to consent for the child(ren) to medical, dental, and surgical treatment during an emergency involving immediate danger to the health and safety of the child(ren); and

(e)   the right to direct the moral and religious training of the child(ren).

IT IS ORDERED AND DECREED that the aforenamed Primary Joint Managing Conservator shall have the exclusive right to establish the primary physical residence of the child(ren) and to receive payments for the support of the child(ren).

IT IS ORDERED AND DECREED that the Primary Joint Managing Conservator shall also have the following rights:

(a)   the right to consent to medical, dental, and surgical treatment of the child(ren) involving invasive procedures, and to psychiatric and psychological treatment;

(b)   the right to receive and give receipt for payments for the support of the child(ren) and to hold or disburse funds for the benefit of the child(ren);

(c)   the right to represent the child(ren) in legal action and to make other decisions of substantial legal significance concerning the child(ren);

(d)   the right to consent to the child(ren)'s marriages and enlistment in the armed forces of the United States;

(e)   the right to make decisions concerning the child(ren)'s education;

(f)   the right to the services and earnings of the child(ren); and

(g)   except when a guardian of the child(ren)'s estates has been appointed, the right to act as an agent of the child(ren) in relation to the child(ren)'s estates if the child(ren)'s action is required by a state, the United States, or a foreign government; and

(h)   the right to inherit from and through the child(ren).

J.   Standard Possession Order.

The Court finds that the provisions of this section comply with the requirements of the Texas Family Code, Chapter 153. IT IS THEREFORE ORDERED AND DECREED that Petitioner and Respondent shall each comply with this Standard Order which is effective immediately and applies to all possessory periods beginning on the date this order is signed by the presiding Judge. IT IS, THEREFORE, ORDERED AND DECREED:

(a)   Mutual Agreement or Specified Terms for Possession.

The aforenamed Joint Managing Conservator shall have possession of the child at times mutually agreed to in advance by the parties and, in the absence of mutual agreement, shall have possession of the child under the specified terms set out in this Standard Order.

(b)   Parents who Reside 100 Miles or Less Apart.

If the Joint Managing Conservator resides 100 miles or less from the primary residence of the child, the Joint Managing Conservator shall have the right to possession of the child as follows:

1.   On weekends beginning at 6:00 P.M. on the first, third, and fifth Friday of each month and ending at 6:00 P.M. on the following Sunday.

2.   If a weekend period of possession of the Joint Managing Conservator coincides with a school holiday during the regular school term or with a federal, state, or local holiday during the summer months in which school is not in session, the weekend possession shall end at 6:00 P.M. on that Monday holiday or school holiday or shall begin at 6:00 P.M. Thursday for a Friday holiday or school holiday, as applicable.

3.   On Wednesday of each week during the regular school term, beginning at 6:00 P.M. and ending at 8:00 P.M.

4.   In even-numbered years beginning at 6:00 P.M. on the day the child is dismissed from school for the Christmas school vacation and ending at noon on December 26.

5.   In odd-numbered years beginning at noon on December 26 and ending at 6:00 P.M. on the day before school resumes after that vacation.

6.   In odd-numbered years beginning at 6:00 P.M. on the day the child is dismissed from school before Thanksgiving and ending at 6:00 P.M. on the following Sunday.

7.   In even-numbered years beginning at 6:00 P.M. on the day the child is dismissed from school for the school's spring vacation and ending at 6:00 P.M. on the day before school resumes after that vacation.

Final Decree of Divorce, Page _____.

80

8.   If the Joint Managing Conservator gives the Primary Joint Managing Conservator written notice by April 1 of each year specifying an extended period or periods of summer possession, the Joint Managing Conservator shall have possession of the child for 30 days beginning not earlier than the day after the child's school is dismissed for the summer vacation and ending not later than 7 days before school resumes at the end of the summer vacation, to be exercised in not more than two separate periods of at least 7 consecutive days each; or

If the Joint Managing Conservator does not give the Primary Joint Managing Conservator written notice by April 1 of each year specifying an extended period or periods of summer possession, the Joint Managing Conservator shall have possession of the child for 30 consecutive days beginning at 6:00 P.M. on July 1 and ending at 6:00 P.M. on July 31.

9.   If the Joint Managing Conservator is not otherwise entitled under this Standard Order to present possession of the child on the child's birthday, the Joint Managing Conservator shall have possession of the child beginning at 6:00 P.M. and ending at 8:00 P.M. on that day, provided that the Joint Managing Conservator picks up the child from the residence of the Primary Joint Managing Conservator and returns the child to that same place.

10.   If a conservator, the father shall have possession of the child beginning at 6:00 P.M. on the Friday preceding Father's Day and ending on Father's Day at 6:00 P.M., provided that, if he is not otherwise entitled under this Standard Order to present possession of the child, he picks up the child from the residence of the Conservator entitled to possession and returns the child to that same place.

11.   If a conservator, the mother shall have possession of the child beginning at 6:00 P.M. on the Friday preceding Mother's Day and ending on Mother's Day at 6:00 P.M., provided that, if she is not otherwise entitled under this Standard Order to present possession of the child, she picks up the child from the residence of the Conservator entitled to possession and returns the child to that same place.

IT IS FURTHER ORDERED AND DECREED that the Primary Joint Managing Conservator shall have a right of possession to the child that is superior to that of the Joint Managing Conservator as follows:

1.   If the Primary Joint Managing Conservator gives the Joint Managing Conservator written notice by April 15 of each year, the Primary Joint Managing Conservator shall have possession of the child on any one weekend beginning at 6:00 P.M. on Friday and ending at 6:00 P.M. on the following Sunday during one period of the Joint Managing Conservator's extended summer possession, provided that the Primary Joint Managing Conservator picks up the child from the Joint Managing Conservator and returns the child to that same place, and

2.   If the Primary Joint Managing Conservator gives the Joint Managing Conservator written notice by April 15 of each year or gives the Joint Managing Conservator 14 days'

written notice on or after April 16 of each year, the Primary Joint Managing Conservator may designate one weekend beginning not earlier than the day after the child's school is dismissed for the summer vacation and ending not later than 7 days before school resumes at the end of the summer vacation, during which an otherwise scheduled weekend period of possession by the Joint Managing Conservator shall not take place, provided that the weekend designated does not interfere with the Joint Managing Conservator's period or periods of extended summer possession or with Father's Day if the Joint Managing Conservator is the father of the child.

3.   If the Primary Joint Managing Conservator is not otherwise entitled under this Standard Order to present possession of the child on the child's birthday, the Primary Joint Managing Conservator shall have possession of the child beginning at 6:00 P.M. and ending at 8:00 P.M. on that day, provided that the Primary Joint Managing Conservator picks up the child from the Joint Managing Conservator's residence and returns the child to that same place.

4.   If a Conservator, the mother shall have possession of the child beginning at 6:00 P.M. on the Friday preceding Mother's Day and ending on Mother's Day at 6:00 P.M., provided that, if she is not otherwise entitled under this Standard Order to present possession of the child, she picks up the child from the residence of the Conservator entitled to possession and returns the child to that same place.

(c)   If the Joint Managing Conservator resides more than 100 miles from the residence of the child, the Joint Managing Conservator shall have the right to possession of the child as follows:

1.   Either regular weekend possession beginning on the first, third, and fifth Friday as provided under the terms applicable to parents who reside 100 miles or less apart or not more than one weekend per month of the Joint Managing Conservator's choice beginning at 6:00 P.M. on the day school recesses for the weekend and ending at 6:00 P.M. on the day before school resumes after the weekend, provided that the Joint Managing Conservator gives the Primary Joint Managing Conservator 14 days' written or telephonic notice preceding a designated weekend, and provided that the Joint Managing Conservator elects an option for this alternative period of possession by written notice given to the Primary Joint Managing Conservator within 90 days after the parties begin to reside more than 100 miles apart, as applicable;

2.   In even-numbered years beginning at 6:00 P.M. on the day the child is dismissed from school for the Christmas school vacation and ending at noon on December 26.

3.   In odd-numbered years beginning at noon on December 26 and ending at 6:00 P.M. on the day before school resumes after that vacation.

4.   In odd-numbered years beginning at 6:00 P.M. on the day the child is dismissed from school before Thanksgiving and ending at 6:00 P.M. on the following Sunday.

5.   Each year beginning at 6:00 P.M. on the day the child is dismissed from school for the school's spring vacation and ending at 6:00 P.M. on the day before school resumes after that vacation.

6.   If the Joint Managing Conservator gives the Primary Joint Managing Conservator written notice by April 1 of each year specifying an extended period or periods of summer possession, the Joint Managing Conservator shall have possession of the child for 42 days beginning not earlier than the day after the child's school is dismissed for the summer vacation and ending not later than 7 days before school resumes at the end of the summer vacation, to be exercised in not more than two separate periods of at least 7 consecutive days each; or

If the Joint Managing Conservator does not give the Primary Joint Managing Conservator written notice by April 1 of each year specifying an extended period or periods of summer possession, the Joint Managing Conservator shall have possession of the child for 42 consecutive days beginning at 6:00 P.M. on June 15 and ending at 6:00 P.M. on July 27 of that year.

7.   If the Joint Managing Conservator is not otherwise entitled under this Standard Order to present possession of a child on the child's birthday, the Joint Managing Conservator shall have possession of a child beginning at 6:00 P.M. and ending at 8:00 P.M. on that day, provided that the Joint Managing Conservator picks up the child from the residence of the Primary Joint Managing Conservator and returns the child to that same place.

8.   If a Conservator, the father shall have possession of the child beginning at 6:00 P.M. on the Friday preceding Father's day and ending on Father's day at 6:00 P.M., provided that, if he is not otherwise entitled under this Standard Order to present possession of the child, he picks up the child from the residence of the Conservator entitled to possession and returns the child to that same place.

9.   If a Conservator, the mother shall have possession of the child beginning at 6:00 P.M. on the Friday preceding Mother's day and ending on Mother's day at 6:00 P.M., provided that, if she is not otherwise entitled under this Standard Order to present possession of the child, she picks up the child from the residence of the Conservator entitled to possession and returns the child to that same place.

IT IS FURTHER ORDERED AND DECREED that the Primary Joint Managing Conservator shall have a right of possession to the child that is superior to that of the Joint Managing Conservator as follows:

1.   If the Primary Joint Managing Conservator gives the Joint Managing Conservator written notice by April 15 of each year, the Primary Joint Managing Conservator shall have possession of the child on one weekend beginning Friday at 6:00 P.M. and ending at 6:00 P.M. on the following Sunday during one period of possession by the Joint Managing Conservator during the Joint Managing Conservator's extended summer possession in that

year, provided that if a period of possession by the Joint Managing Conservator exceeds 30 days, the Primary Joint Managing Conservator may have possession of the child on two nonconsecutive weekends during that time period, and further provided that the Primary Joint Managing Conservator picks up the child from the Joint Managing Conservator and returns the child to that same place; and

2.   If the Primary Joint Managing Conservator gives the Joint Managing Conservator written notice by April 15 of each year, the Primary Joint Managing Conservator may designate 21 days beginning not earlier than the day after the child's school is dismissed for the summer vacation and ending no later than 7 days before school resumes at the end of the summer vacation, to be exercised in not more than two separate periods of at least 7 consecutive days each, during which the Joint Managing Conservator may not have possession of the child, provided that the period or periods so designated do not interfere with the Joint Managing Conservator's period or periods of extended summer possession or with Father's Day if the Joint Managing Conservator is the father of the child.

3.   If the Primary Joint Managing Conservator is not otherwise entitled under this Standard Order to present possession of the child on the child's birthday, the Primary Joint Managing Conservator shall have possession of the child beginning at 6:00 P.M. and ending at 8:00 P.M. on that day, provided that the Primary Joint Managing Conservator picks up the child from the Joint Managing Conservator's residence and returns the child to that same place.

4.   If a Conservator, the mother shall have possession of the child beginning at 6:00 P.M. on the Friday preceding Mother's Day and ending on Mother's Day at 6:00 P.M., provided that, if she is not otherwise entitled under this Standard Order to present possession of the child, she picks up the child from the residence of the Conservator entitled to possession and returns the child to that same place.

(d)   General Terms and Conditions.

IT IS ORDERED AND DECREED that the terms and conditions of possession of the child that apply regardless of the distance between the residence of a parent and the child are as follows:

1.   The Primary Joint Managing Conservator shall surrender the child to the Joint Managing Conservator at the beginning of each period of the Joint Managing Conservator's possession at the residence of the Primary Joint Managing Conservator.

2.   The Joint Managing Conservator shall surrender the child to the Primary Joint Managing Conservator at the end of each period of possession at the residence of the Primary Joint Managing Conservator.

3.   Each conservator shall return with the child the personal effects that the child brought at the beginning of the period of possession.

4.   Either conservator may designate a competent adult to pick up and return the child, as applicable; a conservator or a designated competent adult shall be present when the child is picked up or returned.

5.   A conservator shall give notice to the person in possession of the child on each occasion that the conservator will be unable to exercise that conservator's right of possession for any specified period.

6.   Written notice shall be deemed to have been timely made if received or postmarked before or at the time that notice is due.

7.   Unless provision is made to the contrary herein, all periods of possession shall begin at 6:00 P.M.

8.   If a conservator's time of possession of a child ends at the time school resumes and for any reason the child is not or will not be returned to the school, the conservator in possession of the child shall immediately notify the school and the other conservator that the child will not be or has not been returned to school.

(e)   Definitions:

1.   "School" means the primary or secondary school in which the child is enrolled or, if the child is not enrolled in a primary or secondary school, the public school district in which the child primarily resides.

2.   "Child" means each person under 18 years of age who is not and has not been married or who had the disabilities of minority removed for general purposes who is a subject of this suit, whether one or more.

This concludes the Standard Possession Order.

K.   Duration.

The possession and access ordered above applies to each and every child who is the subject of this suit for so long as that child is under the age of 18 years and not otherwise emancipated.

L.   Child Support.

IT IS ORDERED AND DECREED that _____, hereinafter referred to as "Obligor" for purposes of this child support order, is obligated to pay and, subject to the provisions for withholding from earnings for child support specified below, shall pay to _____ child support of $_____ per month, with the first payment being due and payable on _____, and a like payment being due and payable on the same day of each month thereafter until the first month following the date of the earliest occurrence of one of the following events:

(1)   the youngest child is 18 years or until graduation from high school, whichever is later, provided that, if the child is fully enrolled in an accredited secondary school in a program leading toward a high school diploma, said child support payments shall continue through the end of the month in which the child graduates;

(2)   the youngest child is emancipated through marriage, through removal of the disabilities of minority by court order, or by other operation of law;

(3)   the youngest child dies;

(4)   further order modifying this child support.

M.   <u>Withholding from Earnings.</u>

IT IS ORDERED AND DECREED that any employer of Obligor shall be ordered to withhold from earnings for child support from the disposable earnings of Obligor for the support of the child(ren) of the parties. "Earnings" means compensation paid or payable to Obligor for personal services, whether denominated as wages, salary, compensation received as an independent contractor, overtime pay, severance pay, commission, bonus, or otherwise. The term includes periodic payments pursuant to a pension, an annuity, workers' compensation, a disability and retirement program, and unemployment benefits. "Disposable earnings" is that part of Obligor's earnings remaining after the deduction from those earnings of any amount required by law to be withheld, union dues, nondiscretionary retirement contributions, and medical, hospitalization, and disability insurance coverage for the Obligor and parties' child(ren). Depending on the regularly scheduled wage and salary payments, the employer shall be ordered to withhold from disposable earnings for child support on the schedule appropriate to the employer's payroll period, as follows: $_____ monthly, $_____ semimonthly, $_____ biweekly, or $_____ weekly, provided that the amount of income withheld for child support for any pay period shall not exceed 50 percent of Obligor's disposable earnings. The first payment is due and payable no later than the first pay period following the date on which the "Employer's Order to Withhold Earnings For Child Support" is received by the employer. The employer shall continue to withhold income as long as Obligor remains in employment, and thereafter until the first month following the date of the earliest occurrence of one of the following events:

(1)   the youngest child is 18 years or until graduation from high school, whichever is later, provided that, if the child is fully enrolled in an accredited secondary school in a program leading toward a high school diploma, said child support payments shall continue through the end of the month in which the child graduates;

(2)   the youngest child is emancipated through marriage, through removal of the disabilities of minority by court order, or by operation of law;

(3)   the youngest child dies;

(4)   further order modifying this child support.

13.

IT IS FURTHER ORDERED AND DECREED that all amounts withheld from the disposable earnings of Obligor by the employer and paid in accordance with the order to that employer shall constitute a credit against the child support obligation. If the amount withheld from earnings and credited against the child support obligation is less than 100 percent of the amount ordered to be paid, the balance due remains an obligation of Obligor, and it is hereby ORDERED AND DECREED that Obligor pay the balance due directly to the registry of the court as set forth below.

On this date the Court signed an "Employer's Order To Withhold Earnings For Child Support."

N.   IT IS FURTHER ORDERED AND DECREED that all child support payments shall be made through the _____ County Child Support Office and subsequently remitted by that office to _____ for the child(ren)'s support.

O.   IT IS FURTHER ORDERED AND DECREED that Obligor and Obligee shall each pay to the _____ County Child Support Office, the amount of $_____ annually. The first such payment in the amount of $_____ is due and payable on _____, and a payment of $_____ shall be due and payable on the _____ day of _____ of each year thereafter, until the date of the earliest occurrence of one of the following events:

(1)   the youngest child is 18 years or until graduation from high school, whichever is later, provided that, if the child is fully enrolled in an accredited secondary school in a program leading toward a high school diploma, said child support payments shall continue through the end of the month in which the child graduates;

(2)   the youngest child is emancipated through marriage, through removal of the disabilities of minority by court order, or by operation of law;

(3)   the youngest child dies;

(4)   further order modifying this child support.

P.   IT IS FURTHER ORDERED AND DECREED that Obligor shall notify this Court and _____ by certified mail, return receipt requested, of any address changes and of any employment termination. This notice shall be given within 7 days after the address change or the employment termination. This and any subsequent notice shall also provide the current address of Obligor and the name and address of Obligor's current employer.

IT IS ORDERED AND DECREED that, on the request of a prosecuting attorney, the Attorney General, the Petitioner, or the Respondent, the Clerk of this Court shall cause a certified copy of the "Employer's Order To Withhold Earnings For Child Support" to be delivered to any employer. IT IS FURTHER ORDERED AND DECREED that the Clerk of this Court shall attach a copy of Chapter 158, Subchapter C of the Texas Family Code for the information of any employer.

Q.   Health Care.

IT IS ORDERED AND DECREED that health insurance for the child(ren) shall be provided as follows:

1.   _____, hereinafter referred to as "Obligor", shall provide health insurance for the child(ren) through (1) coverage available through Obligor's employment or membership in a union, trade association, or other organization, or (2) coverage available to _____, hereinafter referred to as "Obligee", through Obligee's employment or membership in a union, trade association, or other organization, or (3) the purchase and maintenance of health insurance coverage as set out below.

2.   "Health insurance" means insurance coverage that provides basic health care services, including usual physician services, office visits, hospitalization, and laboratory, X-ray, and emergency services that may be provided through a health maintenance organization or other private or public organization.

3.   If health insurance is available for the child(ren) through Obligor's employment, Obligor shall, at Obligor's sole cost, keep in full force health insurance coverage through Obligor's employer or membership in a union, trade association, or other organization.

4.   If health insurance for the child(ren)is not available to Obligor through Obligor's employment or membership in a union, trade association, or other organization but is available to Obligee through Obligee's employment or membership in a union, trade association, or other organization, Obligee shall have the child(ren) covered on Obligee's health insurance plan and Obligor shall pay to Obligee directly the cost of insuring the child(ren) on Obligee's health insurance plan on the first day of each month after Obligor receives demand from Obligee for payment.

5.   If the conservator through whose employment health insurance for the child(ren) has been provided is terminating that employment or health insurance will not be available for the child(ren) through either parties' employment, the party leaving employment or losing coverage shall, within 10 days of termination of his or her employment or health insurance coverage, convert the health insurance policy to an individual policy of coverage for the child(ren) in an amount at least equal to the coverage that ended or will end. Also, if that health insurance was available through Obligee's employment or membership in a union, trade association, or other organization, Obligor shall reimburse Obligee for the cost of the converted policy as set forth above.

6.   If the health insurance policy covering the child(ren) cannot be converted and if no health insurance is available for the child(ren) through either parties employment, Obligor shall purchase and keep at Obligor's sole cost, health insurance coverage for the child(ren). Obligor shall provide verification of the purchase of said insurance to Obligee at Obligee's last known address, including the insurance certificate number and the plan summary, no later than 10 days following the issuance of the policy.

7.   The party who is not carrying the health insurance for the child(ren) shall give to the party carrying the health insurance all forms, receipts, and statements indicating the health care expenses the party not carrying the health insurance incurs for the child(ren) within 10 days. The parent who is carrying the health insurance for the child(ren) shall submit all forms to the insurance company for payment of health care expenses incurred for the children to the insurer within 10 days of that party receiving any form, receipt, or statement reflecting the expense.

8.   Obligor is also ORDERED AND DECREED to pay, and shall pay 50% of all uninsured health care expenses incurred by or for the parties' child(ren), including any deductibles, prescription drugs, psychiatric care, dental, and eye care expenses, for as long as child support is to be paid under this decree and Obligee is ORDERED AND DECREED to pay, and shall pay 50% of all uninsured health care expenses incurred by or for the parties' child(ren), including any deductibles, prescription drugs, psychiatric care, dental, and eye care expenses, for as long as child support is to be paid under this decree.

9.   The party who paid for a health care expense for the child(ren) must submit to the other party all forms, receipts, and statements indicating the uninsured part of the health care expenses the paying party incurs for the child(ren) within 10 days after he or she receives them. Within 10 days after the nonpaying party receives the forms, receipts, or statements, that party will pay his or her share of the uninsured part of the health care expenses by paying the health care provider directly or by reimbursing the paying party for any advance payment above the paying party's share of the expenses.

10.   Obligor shall furnish to Obligee the following information not later than the 30th day after the date the notice of the rendition of this order is received:

(a)   Obligor's Social Security number;

(b)   the name and address of Obligor's employer;

(c)   whether the employer is self-insured or has health insurance available;

(d)   proof that health insurance has been provided for the child(ren); and

(e)   the name of the health insurance carrier, the number of the policy, a copy of the policy and schedule of benefits, a health insurance membership card, claim forms, and any other information necessary to submit a claim or, if the employer is self-insured, a copy of the schedule of benefits, a membership card, claim forms, and any other information necessary to submit a claim.

11.   If the health insurance for the child(ren) lapses or terminates, Obligor must notify Obligee not later than the 15th day after the date of termination or lapse and the availability of additional health insurance to the Obligor after the termination or lapse of coverage no later than the 15th day after the date the insurance becomes available. Obligor must enroll the child(ren) in a health insurance plan at the next available enrollment period.

12.   **WARNING:**

A PARENT ORDERED TO PROVIDE HEALTH INSURANCE WHO FAILS TO DO SO IS LIABLE FOR NECESSARY MEDICAL EXPENSES OF THE CHILD(REN), WITHOUT REGARD TO WHETHER THE EXPENSES WOULD HAVE BEEN PAID IF HEALTH INSURANCE HAD BEEN PROVIDED AND THE COST OF HEALTH INSURANCE PREMIUMS OR CONTRIBUTIONS, IF ANY PAID ON BEHALF OF THE CHILD(REN).

IT IS FURTHER ORDERED AND DECREED that the child support as set forth herein shall be discharged only in the manner ordered.

Each party to this cause is ORDERED AND DECREED to inform the other party to this cause, in writing, of his or her current residence address, mailing address, home telephone number, name of employer, address of employment, and work telephone number and of the address of the child(ren)'s school or day-care center. Each party who intends a change of place of residence, mailing address, home telephone number, name of employer, address of employment, and work telephone number is ORDERED AND DECREED to give notice of the intended dates of changes, along with the actual changes to the Clerk of this Court and to the other party the 60th day before the date the party intends to make the change or, if the party did not know and could not have known of the change within the 60-day period, on the 5th day after the date the party knew of the change.

WARNING

FAILURE TO OBEY A COURT ORDER FOR CHILD SUPPORT OR FOR POSSESSION OF OR ACCESS TO A CHILD MAY RESULT IN FURTHER LITIGATION TO ENFORCE THE ORDER, INCLUDING CONTEMPT OF COURT. A FINDING OF CONTEMPT MAY BE PUNISHED BY CONFINEMENT IN JAIL FOR UP TO SIX MONTHS, A FINE OF UP TO $500 FOR EACH VIOLATION, AND A MONEY JUDGMENT FOR PAYMENT OF ATTORNEY'S FEES AND COURT COSTS.

FAILURE OF A PARTY TO MAKE A CHILD SUPPORT PAYMENT TO THE PLACE AND IN THE MANNER REQUIRED BY A COURT ORDER MAY RESULT IN THE PARTY'S NOT RECEIVING CREDIT FOR MAKING THE PAYMENT.

FAILURE OF A PARTY TO PAY CHILD SUPPORT DOES NOT JUSTIFY DENYING THAT PARTY COURT-ORDERED POSSESSION OF OR ACCESS TO A CHILD. REFUSAL BY A PARTY TO ALLOW POSSESSION OF OR ACCESS TO A CHILD DOES NOT JUSTIFY FAILURE TO PAY COURT-ORDERED CHILD SUPPORT TO THAT PARTY. EACH PERSON WHO IS A PARTY TO THIS ORDER OR DECREE IS ORDERED TO NOTIFY EACH OTHER PARTY WITHIN TEN DAYS AFTER THE DATE OF ANY CHANGE IN THE PARTY'S CURRENT RESIDENCE ADDRESS, MAILING ADDRESS, HOME TELEPHONE NUMBER, NAME OF EMPLOYER, ADDRESS OF EMPLOYMENT, AND WORK TELEPHONE NUMBER. THE PARTY IS ORDERED TO GIVE NOTICE OF AN INTENDED CHANGE IN ANY OF THE REQUIRED INFORMATION TO EACH OTHER PARTY ON OR BEFORE THE 60TH DAY BEFORE THE INTENDED CHANGE. IF THE PARTY DOES NOT KNOW OR COULD NOT HAVE KNOWN OF THE CHANGE IN SUFFICIENT TIME TO PROVIDE 60-DAY NOTICE, THE PARTY IS ORDERED TO GIVE NOTICE OF THE CHANGE ON OR BEFORE THE FIFTH DAY AFTER THE DATE THAT THE PARTY KNOWS OF THE CHANGE.

ALL NOTICES SHALL BE IN WRITING AND SHALL STATE THE NEW INFORMATION AND THE EFFECTIVE DATE OF THE CHANGE. THE DUTY TO FURNISH THIS INFORMATION TO EACH OTHER PARTY CONTINUES AS LONG AS ANY PERSON, BY VIRTUE OF THIS ORDER OR DECREE, IS UNDER AN OBLIGATION TO PAY CHILD SUPPORT OR IS ENTITLED TO POSSESSION OF OR ACCESS TO A CHILD.

FAILURE BY A PARTY TO OBEY THE ORDER OF THIS COURT TO PROVIDE EACH OTHER PARTY WITH THE CHANGE IN THE REQUIRED INFORMATION MAY RESULT IN FURTHER LITIGATION TO ENFORCE THE ORDER, INCLUDING CONTEMPT OF COURT. A FINDING OF CONTEMPT MAY BE PUNISHED BY CONFINEMENT IN JAIL FOR UP TO SIX MONTHS, A FINE OF UP TO $500 FOR EACH VIOLATION, AND A MONEY JUDGMENT FOR PAYMENT OF ATTORNEY'S FEES AND COURT COSTS.

R.   Division of Marital Estate.

The parties have agreed and the Court therefore finds that the following division of the parties' marital estate is just and right.

S.   IT IS THEREFORE ORDERED AND DECREED that Petitioner is awarded as Petitioner's sole property the following:

1.   All personal property and effects that are currently in the possession of Petitioner or subject to Petitioner's sole control, unless express provision is made in this decree to the contrary.

2.   Any and all stocks, bonds, and securities registered in Petitioner's name.

3.   Any and all money on account in any financial institution in Petitioner's name.

4.   All sums and proceeds from and to any and all employee benefit programs, retirement plans and any other plans existing because of Petitioner's past, present, or future employment unless express provision is made in this decree to the contrary.

5.   All policies of life insurance with cash values insuring the Petitioner's life.

6.

IT IS FURTHER ORDERED AND DECREED that Respondent is divested of all claims and interest in and right and title to the above property awarded to Petitioner.

T.   IT IS FURTHER ORDERED AND DECREED that Respondent is awarded as Respondent's sole property the following:

1.   All personal property and effects that are currently in the possession of Respondent or subject to Respondent's sole control, unless express provision is made in this decree to the contrary.

2.   Any and all stocks, bonds, and securities registered in Respondent's name.

3.   Any and all money on account in any financial institution in Respondent's name.

4.   All sums and proceeds from and to any and all employee benefit programs, retirement plans and any other plans existing because of Respondent's past, present, or future employment unless express provision is made in this decree to the contrary.

5.   All policies of life insurance, with cash values, insuring the Respondent's life.

6.

IT IS FURTHER ORDERED AND DECREED that Petitioner is divested of all claims and interest in and right and title to the above property awarded to Respondent.

U.   Petitioner IS ORDERED AND DECREED to pay the following debts and shall indemnify and hold Respondent and Respondent's property harmless from any failure to pay these debts:

1.   All debts and other obligations incurred in Petitioner's name or solely by Petitioner after the parties' date of separation unless express provision is made in this decree to the contrary.

2.

V.   Respondent IS ORDERED AND DECREED to pay the following debts and shall indemnify and hold Petitioner and Petitioner's property harmless from any failure to pay these debts:

1.   All debts and other obligations incurred in Respondent's name or solely by Respondent after the parties' date of separation unless express provision is made in this decree to the contrary.

2.

W.   Court Cost.

Court costs are to be borne by the party who incurred said costs.

X.   Clarifying Orders

The right to make orders necessary to clarify and enforce this decree is expressly reserved by this court and such reservation and right does not affect the finality of this decree.

Y.   IT IS ORDERED AND DECREED that _____'s
name is hereby changed to _____.

Z.   Relief Not Granted

IT IS ORDERED AND DECREED that all relief requested in this cause and not expressly
granted is denied.

Date of Judgement

SIGNED on _____, _____.

_____
JUDGE PRESIDING

APPROVED AND CONSENTED TO:

_____   _____
Petitioner   Respondent

Y.   <u>Relief Not Granted</u>

IT IS ORDERED AND DECREED that all relief requested in this cause and not expressly granted is denied.

<u>Date of Judgement</u>

SIGNED on _____, _____.

_____
JUDGE PRESIDING

APPROVED AND CONSENTED TO:

_____   _____
Petitioner   Respondent

APPENDIX A

The Pauper's Oath

If you believe that you cannot afford to pay the filing fees for your divorce, you may fill out one of the following forms and present it to the clerk of the court when you file for your divorce. There is a form for a divorce without children and a form for a divorce with children. Be sure to complete the correct form.

Rule 145 of the Texas Rules of Civil Procedure provides for the Pauper's Oath, more specifically identified as an Affidavit of Inability. Such an affidavit "shall contain complete information as to the party's identity, nature and amount of governmental entitlement income, nature and amount of employment income, other income, (interest, dividends, etc.), spouse's income if available to the party, property owned (other than homestead), cash or checking account, dependents, debts, and monthly expenses."

Fill in the blanks with the information requested and place a check mark in front of the statement or statements that apply to you. If you place a check mark in front of a statement and that statement has blank lines in it, please be sure to fill in those blank lines that apply.

After you have filled out the form, it must be signed in the presence of a notary public.

CAUSE NO. _____

IN THE MATTER OF THE MARRIAGE	X	IN THE DISTRICT COURT OF
OF	X	
_____	X	_____COUNTY, TEXAS
	X	
AND	X	
_____	X	_____ JUDICIAL DISTRICT

AFFIDAVIT OF INABILITY

THE STATE OF TEXAS   X

COUNTY OF _____ X

A.   BEFORE ME, the undersigned authority, appeared

_____, Petitioner, in person, who, after being duly sworn, on

oath stated:

B.   "My name is _____. I am the Petitioner in this cause.

C.   I am unable to pay the court costs because:

_____ I own no property other than my personal effects.

_____ I have _____ dependents.

_____ I am unemployed.

_____ My monthly income is $_____ from _____
_____.

_____ I currently have $_____ in cash and in a checking account.

_____ I have no income from any other sources.

_____ I have a total monthly debt of $_____.

100

_____ My spouse does not give me any money."

                                                     _____

                                                     Petitioner

SUBSCRIBED AND SWORN TO BEFORE me this _____ day of _____, _____.

                                                     _____

                                                     Notary Public

CAUSE NO._____

IN THE MATTER OF THE MARRIAGE OF	X	IN THE DISTRICT COURT
_____ AND	X	
_____	X	_____ JUDICIAL DISTRICT
AND IN THE INTEREST OF		
_____	X	
_____		
_____	X	
_____		
_____ ,		
CHILD(REN)	X	_____COUNTY, TEXAS

AFFIDAVIT OF INABILITY

THE STATE OF TEXAS   X
COUNTY OF _____   X

A.   BEFORE ME, the undersigned authority, appeared

_____, Petitioner, in person, who, after being duly sworn, on

oath stated:

B.   "My name is _____. I am the Petitioner in this cause.

C.   I am unable to pay the court costs because:

      _____ I own no property other than my personal effects.

      _____ I have _____ dependents.

102

_____ I am unemployed.

_____ My monthly income is $_____ from _____
_____.

_____ I currently have $_____ in cash and in a checking account.

_____ I have no income from any other sources.

_____ I have a total monthly debt of $_____.

_____ My spouse does not give me any money."

_____
Petitioner

SUBSCRIBED AND SWORN TO BEFORE me this _____ day of _____,
_____.

_____
Notary Public

APPENDIX B

DISTRICT CLERKS

STATE OF TEXAS

Anderson County
Maxine Barnette
P O Box 1159
Palestine TX 75802-1159
903/723-7443

Andrews County
Cynthia Jones
P O Box 328
Andrews TX 79714-0328
915/524-1417

Angelina County
Jimmie F. Robinson
P O Box 908
Lufkin TX 75902-0908
936/634-4312

Aransas County
Pam Heard
301 N Live Oak
Rockport TX 78382-2798
361/790-0128

Archer County
Jane Ham
P O Box 815
Archer City TX 76351
940/574-4615

Armstrong County
Joe Reck
P O Box 309
Claude TX 79019-0309
806/226-2081

Atascosa County
Jerome T. Brite
Courthouse Cir, No 52
Jourdanton TX 78026
830/769-3011

Austin County
Marie Myers
One E Main
Bellville TX 77418-1598
979/865-5911

Bailey County
Elaine Parker
300 S 1st
Muleshoe TX 79347
806/272-3165

Bandera County
Tammy Kneuper
P O Box 2688
Bandera TX 78003-2688
830/796-4606

Bastrop County
La Nelle Hibbs
P O Box 770
Bastrop TX 78602
512/332-7244

Baylor County
Doris Rushing
P O Box 689
Seymour TX 76380-0689
940/889-3322

Bee County
Sandra Clark
P O Box 666
Beeville TX 78104-0666
361/362-3242

Bell County
Shelia Norman
P O Box 909
Belton TX 76513-0909
254/933-5197

Bexar County
Reagan E. Greer
100 Dolorosa
San Antonio TX 78205
210/335-2113

Blanco County
Dorothy Uecker
P O Box 65
Johnson City TX 78636
830/868-7357

Borden County
Joyce Herridge
P O Box 124
Gail TX 79738
806/756-4312

Bosque County
Sandra L. Woosley
P O Box 674
Meridian TX 76665
254/435-2334

Bowie County
Billy Fox
P O Box 248
New Boston TX 75570
903/628-6775

Brazoria County
Jerry Deere
111 E Locust
Angleton TX 77515-4678
979/864-1316

Brazos County
Marc Hamlin
300 E 26th St, Ste 216
Bryan TX 77803-5360
979/361-4230

Brewster County
Jo Ann Salgado
P O Box 1024
Alpine TX 79831
915/837-6216

Briscoe County
Bena Hester
P O Box 555
Silverton TX 79257
806/823-2134

Brooks County
Noe Guerra, Jr.
P O Box 534
Falfurrias TX 78355
361/325-5604

Brown County
Jan Brown
200 S Broadway
Brownwood TX 76801-
915/646-5514

Burleson County
Doris H. Brewer
100 W Buck St, Ste 303
Caldwell TX 77836
979/567-2336

Burnet County
Kathy Barrow
220 S Pierce
Burnet TX 78611-3136
512/756-5454

Caldwell County
Emma Jean Schulle
P O Box 749
Lockhart TX 78644-0749
512/398-1805

Calhoun County
Pamela Martin Hartgrove
Co Courthouse
Port Lavaca TX 77979
361/553-4630

Callahan County
Sharon Owens
104 W 4th St, Ste 300
Baird TX 79504-5396
915/854-1800

Cameron County
Aurora De La Garza
974 E Harrison
Brownsville TX 78520
956/544-0838

Camp County
Doloria A. Bradshaw
126 Church St
Pittsburg TX 75686
903/856-3221

Carson County
Sonya Shieldknight
P O Box 487
Panhandle TX 79068
806/537-3873

Cass County
Becky Wilbanks
P O Box 510
Linden TX 75563-0510
903/756-7514

Castro County
Joyce Thomas
100 E Bedford, Rm 101
Dimmitt TX 79027
806/647-3338

Chambers County
R. B. Scherer, Jr.
P O Box NN
Anahuac TX 77514-1739
409/267-8276

Cherokee County
Marlys Sue Mason
P O Drawer C
Rusk TX 75785-0505
903/683-6908

Childress County
Zona Prince
Co Courthouse, Box 4
Childress TX 79201
940/937-6143

Clay County
Dan Slagle
P O Box 568
Henrietta TX 76365-0568
940/538-4561

Cochran County
Rita Tyson
Co Courthouse, Rm 102
Morton TX 79346-2500
806/266-5450

Coke County
Mary Grim
P O Box 150
Robert Lee TX 76945
915/453-2631

Coleman County
Jo Chapman
P O Box 512
Coleman TX 76834-0512
915/625-2568

Collin County
Hannah Kunkle
P O Box 578
McKinney TX 75070-0578
972/548-4320

Collingsworth County
Jackie Johnson
800 W Ave, Box 10
Wellington TX 79095
806/447-2408

Colorado County
Harvey Vornsand
400 Spring St, Rm 210E
Columbus TX 78934
979/732-2536

Comal County
Margaret Herbrich
150 N Seguin, Ste 304
New Braunfels TX 78130
830/620-5574

Comanche County
LaNell Williams
P O Box 206
Comanche TX 76442
915/356-2342

Concho County
Barbara K. Hoffman
P O Box 98
Paint Rock TX 76866
915/732-4322

Cooke County
Patricia A. Payne
Co Courthouse
Gainesville TX 76240
940/668-5450

Coryell County
Janice M. May
P O Box 4
Gatesville TX 76528
254/865-5911

Cottle County
Beckey J. Tucker
P O Box 717
Paducah TX 79248-0717
806/492-3823

Crane County
Judy Crawford
P O Box 578
Crane TX 79731-0578
915/558-3581

Crockett County
Debbi Puckett
P O Drawer C
Ozona TX 76943
915/392-2022

Crosby County
Karla Isbell
201 W Aspen, Ste 207
Crosbyton TX 79322
806/675-2071

Culberson County
Linda McDonald
P O Box 158
Van Horn TX 79855
915/283-2058

Dallam County
LuAnn Taylor
P O Box 1352
Dalhart TX 79022
806/249-4751

Dallas County
Jim Hamlin
600 Commerce
Dallas TX 75202-4606
214/653-7149

Dawson County
Carolyn L. Turner
P O Box 1268
Lamesa TX 79331-1268
806/872-7373

De Witt County
Tabeth Ruschhaupt
P O Box 845
Cuero TX 77954
361/275-2221

Deaf Smith County
Jean Schumacher
235 E 3rd, Rm 304
Hereford TX 79045-5593
806/364-3901

Delta County
Carolyn Yeager Anglin
P O Box 455
Cooper TX 75432-0455
903/395-4110

Denton County
Sherri Adelstein
P O Box 2146
Denton TX 76209
940/565-8530

Dickens County
Winona Humphreys
P O Box 120
Dickens TX 79229
806/623-5531

Dimmit County
Alicia Lopez Martinez
103 N 5th
Carrizo Springs TX 78834
830/876-2323

Donley County
Fay Vargas
P O Drawer U
Clarendon TX 79226
806/874-3436

Duval County
Richard Barton
P O Drawer 428
San Diego TX 78384
361/279-3322

Eastland County
Bill Miears
P O Box 670
Eastland TX 76448
254/629-2664

Ector County
Jackie Sue Barnes
300 N Grant, Rm 301
Odessa TX 79761-5170
915/498-4290

Edwards County
Sarah McNealy
P O Box 184
Rocksprings TX 78880
830/683-2235

El Paso County
Edie Rubalcaba
500 E San Antonio
El Paso TX 79901-2489
915/546-2021

Ellis County
Billie Fuller
1201 N Hwy 77, Ste B
Waxahachie TX 75165
972/923-5000

Erath County
Thomas Pack
Co Courthouse Annex
Stephenville TX 76401
254/965-1486

Falls County
Larry R. Hoelscher
P O Box 229
Marlin TX 76661-0229
254/883-1419

Fannin County
Rochelle Turner
Co Courthouse
Bonham TX 75418-4346
903/583-7459

Fayette County
Virginia Wied
Co Courthouse
La Grange TX 78945
979/968-3548

Fisher County
Bettie Hargrove
P O Box 88
Roby TX 79543-0088
915/776-2279

Floyd County
Barbara Edwards
P O Box 67
Floydada TX 79235
806/983-4923

Foard County
Sherry Weatherred
P O Box 539
Crowell TX 79227-0539
940/684-1365

Fort Bend County
Glory Hopkins
301 Jackson
Richmond TX 77469
281/344-3953

Franklin County
Barbara Keith Campbell
P O Box 68
Mount Vernon TX 75457
903/537-4786

Freestone County
Janet Haydon Chappell
P O Box 722
Fairfield TX 75840-0722
903/389-2534

Frio County
Ramona B. Rodriguez
500 E San Antonio St, #8
Pearsall TX 78061-3100
830/334-8073

Gaines County
Virginia Stewart
101 S Main, Rm 213
Seminole TX 79360
915/758-4014

Galveston County
Evelyn Wells Robison
722 Moody, 4th Fl
Galveston TX 77550
409/766-2424

Garza County
Jerry Hays
P O Box 366
Post TX 79356-0366
806/495-4430

Gillespie County
Barbara Meyer
101 W Main St, No 204
Fredericksburg TX
78624
830/997-6517

Glasscock County
Rebecca Batla
P O Box 190
Garden City TX 79739
915/354-2371

Goliad County
Gail M. Turley
P O Box 50
Goliad TX 77963-0050
361/645-3294

Gonzales County
Patricia Heinemeyer
P O Box 34
Gonzales TX 78629-0034
830/672-2326

Gray County
Gaye Honderich
P O Box 1139
Pampa TX 79066-1139
806/669-8010

Grayson County
Cyndi Mathis-Spencer
200 S Crockett, Ste 120-A
Sherman TX 75090
903/813-4352

Gregg County
Ruby Cooper
P O Box 711
Longview TX 75606-0711
903/237-2663

Grimes County
Wayne Rucker
P O Box 234
Anderson TX 77830-0234
936/873-2111

Guadalupe County
James Behrendt
101 E Court
Seguin TX 78155-5742
830/303-4188

Hale County
Anna Evans
500 Broadway, Rm 200
Plainview TX 79072-8050
806/291-5226

Hall County
Raye Bailey
Co Courthouse, 512 Main,
Ste 8
Memphis TX 79245-3343
806/259-2627

116

Hamilton County
Leoma Larance
Co Courthouse
Hamilton TX 76531
254/386-3417

Hansford County
Kim V. Vera
P O Box 397
Spearman TX 79081
806/659-4110

Hardeman County
Judy Cokendolpher
P O Box 30
Quanah TX 79252-0030
940/663-2961

Hardin County
Vicki Johnson
P O Box 2997
Kountze TX 77625-2997
409/246-5150

Harris County
Charles Bacarisse
301 Fannin, Room 400
Houston TX 77002
713/755-5711

Harrison County
Sherry Griffis
P O Box 1119
Marshall TX 75671-1119
903/935-4845

Hartley County
Diane Thompson
P O Box Q
Channing TX 79018-0997
806/235-3582

Haskell County
Penny Young Anderson
P O Box 27
Haskell TX 79521-0027
940/864-2030

Hays County
Cecelia Adair
110 E MLK Dr, Rm 123
San Marcos TX 78666
512/393-7660

Hemphill County
Charles M. Cole
P O Box 867
Canadian TX 79014-0867
806/323-6212

Henderson County
Betty Ramsey
Co Courthouse
Athens TX 75751
903/675-6115

Hidalgo County
Pauline G. Gonzalez
100 N Closner, 1st Fl
Edinburg TX 78539
956/318-2200

Hill County
Charlotte Barr
P O Box 634
Hillsboro TX 76645-0634
254/582-4042

Hockley County
Dennis Price
802 Houston St, Ste 316
Levelland TX 79336-4545
806/894-8527

Hood County
Tonna Trumble
Co Courthouse, Rm 21
Granbury TX 76048
817/579-3236

Hopkins County
Patricia Dorner
P O Box 391
Sulphur Springs TX
903/438-4081

Houston County
Pam Pugh
P O Box 1186
Crockett TX 75835
936/544-3255

Howard County
Glenda Brasel
P O Drawer 2138
Big Spring TX 79721
915/264-2223

Hudspeth County
Patricia Bramblett
P O Drawer 58
Sierra Blanca TX 79851
915/369-2301

Hunt County
Ann Prince
P O Box 1437
Greenville TX 75403
903/408-4172

Hutchinson County
Joan Carder
P O Box 580
Stinnett TX 79083-0580
806/878-4017

Irion County
Reba Criner
P O Box 736
Mertzon TX 76941-0736
915/835-2421

Jack County
Lelia Vene Cozart
100 Main St
Jacksboro TX 76458
940/567-2141

Jackson County
Sharon Mathis Whittley
115 W Main, Rm 203
Edna TX 77957-2793
361/782-3812

Jasper County
Linda Ryall
P O Box 2088
Jasper TX 75951
409/384-9644

Jeff Davis County
Sue Blackley
P O Box 398
Fort Davis TX 79734
915/426-3251

Jefferson County
Johnny Appleman
P O Box 3707
Beaumont TX 77704
409/835-8580

Jim Hogg County
Pamela L. Benavides
P O Box 878
Hebbronville TX 78361
361/527-4031

Jim Wells County
R. David Guerrero
P O Drawer 2219
Alice TX 78333-2219
361/668-5717

Johnson County
David Lloyd
P O Box 495
Cleburne TX 76033
817/556-6836

Jones County
Nona Carter
P O Box 308
Anson TX 79501-0308
915/823-3731

Karnes County
Patricia Brysch
101 N Panna Maria, #2
Karnes City TX 78118
830/780-2562

Kaufman County
Sandra Featherston
100 W Mulberry
Kaufman TX 75142-2087
972/932-4331

Kendall County
Shirley R. Stehling
201 E San Antonio, #201
Boerne TX 78006-2032
830/249-9343

Kenedy County
Barbara B. Turcotte
P O Box 227
Sarita TX 78385-0227
361/294-5220

Kent County
Rena Jones
P O Box 9
Jayton TX 79528-0009
806/237-3881

Kerr County
Linda Uecker
700 Main St
Kerrville TX 78028
830/792-2281

Kimble County
Elaine Carpenter
501 Main St
Junction TX 76849-4763
915/446-3353

King County
Linda Lewis
P O Box 135
Guthrie TX 79236-0135
806/596-4412

Kinney County
Dora Elia Sandoval
P O Drawer 9
Brackettville TX 78832
830/563-2521

Kleberg County
Martha I. Soliz
P O Box 312
Kingsville TX 78364-0312
361/595-8561

Knox County
Ronnie Verhalen
P O Box 196
Benjamin TX 79505-0196
940/454-2441

La Salle County
Peggy Murray
P O Box 340
Cotulla TX 78014-0340
830/879-4434

Lamar County
Marvin Ann Patterson
119 N Main St, Rm 306
Paris TX 75460-4267
903/737-2427

Lamb County
Celia Kuykendall
100 6th St, Rm 212
Littlefield TX 79339-3366
806/385-4222

Lampasas County
Terri Cox
P O Box 327
Lampasas TX 76550
512/556-8271

Lavaca County
Calvin J. Albrecht
P O Box 306
Hallettsville TX 77964
361/798-2351

Lee County
Adeline Melcher
P O Box 176
Giddings TX 78942
979/542-2947

Leon County
Gloria McCarty
P O Box 39
Centerville TX 75833
903/536-2227

Liberty County
Melody Gilmore
1923 Sam Houston #303
Liberty TX 77575-4847
936/336-4682

Limestone County
Peggy Murray Hill
P O Box 230
Groesbeck TX 76642
254/729-3206

Lipscomb County
Terri Parker
P O Box 70
Lipscomb TX 79056-0070
806/862-3091

Live Oak County
Lois Shannon
P O Box 440
George West TX 78022
361/449-2733

Llano County
Debbie Honig
P O Box 877
Llano TX 78643-0877
915/247-5036

Loving County
Beverly Hanson
P O Box 194
Mentone TX 79754-0194
915/377-2441

Lubbock County
Jean Anne Stratton
P O Box 10536
Lubbock TX 79408-3536
806/775-1317

Lynn County
Sandra Laws
P O Box 939
Tahoka TX 79373-0939
806/998-4274

Madison County
Joyce C. Batson
101 W Main, Rm 226
Madisonville TX 77864
936/348-9203

Marion County
Janie McCay
P O Box 628
Jefferson TX 75657
903/665-2441

Martin County
Susie Hull
P O Box 906
Stanton TX 79782-0906
915/756-3412

Mason County
Beatrice Langehennig
P O Box 702
Mason TX 76856-0702
915/347-5253

Matagorda County
Becky Denn
1700 7th St, Rm 307
Bay City TX 77414-5092
979/244-7621

Maverick County
Irene Rodriguez
P O Box 3659
Eagle Pass TX 78853
830/773-2629

McCulloch County
Mackye Johnson
Co Courthouse, Rm 205
Brady TX 76825
915/597-0733

McLennan County
Joe Johnson
P O Box 2451
Waco TX 76703-2451
254/757-5054

McMullen County
Nell Hodgin
P O Box 235
Tilden TX 78072-0235
361/274-3215

Medina County
M. Eva Soto
1100 16th St, Rm 209
Hondo TX 78861
830/741-6000

Menard County
Elsie Maserang
P O Box 1028
Menard TX 76859
915/396-4682

Midland County
Vivian Wood
200 W Wall, Ste 301
Midland TX 79701-4557
915/688-1234

Milam County
Betty Robertson
P O Box 999
Cameron TX 76520-0999
254/697-7053

Mills County
Beulah L. Roberts
P O Box 646
Goldthwaite TX 76844
915/648-2711

Mitchell County
Sharon Hammond
Co Courthouse, Rm 302
Colorado City TX 79512
915/728-5918

Montague County
Condell Lowrie
P O Box 155
Montague TX 76251
940/894-2571

Montgomery County
Barbara Gladden-Adamick
P O Box 2985
Conroe TX 77305-2985
936/539-7855

Moore County
Diane Hoefling
715 S Dumas Ave, #109
Dumas TX 79029-4326
806/935-4218

Morris County
Gwen Oney
500 Broadnax St
Daingerfield TX 75638
903/645-2321

Motley County
Lucretia Campbell
P O Box 660
Matador TX 79244
806/347-2621

Nacogdoches County
Shelby Solomon
101 W Main
Nacogdoches TX 75961
936/560-7730

Navarro County
Marilyn Greer
P O Box 1439
Corsicana TX 75151
903/654-3041

Newton County
Abbie N. Stark
P O Box 535
Newton TX 75966-0535
409/379-3951

Nolan County
Vera Holloman
100 E 3rd, Ste 200
Sweetwater TX 79556
915/235-2111

Nueces County
Oscar Soliz
901 Leopard, Ste 313
Corpus Christi TX 78401
361/888-0450

Ochiltree County
Shawn Bogard
511 S Main
Perryton TX 79070
806/435-8054

Oldham County
Becky Groneman
P O Box 360
Vega TX 79092-0360
806/267-2667

Orange County
Vickie Edgerly
P O Box 427
Orange TX 77631-0427
409/882-7028

Palo Pinto County
Helen Slemmons
P O Box 189
Palo Pinto TX 76484
940/659-1222

Panola County
Sandra King
Co Courthouse, Rm 227
Carthage TX 75633
903/693-0306

Parker County
Elvera M. Johnson
P O Box 340
Weatherford TX 76086
817/598-6111

Parmer County
Sandra Warren
P O Box 195
Farwell TX 79325-0195
806/481-3419

Pecos County
Kaye Creech
400 S Nelson
Fort Stockton TX 79735
915/336-3503

Polk County
Kathy Clifton
101 W Church St
Livingston TX 77351
936/327-6814

Potter County
Caroline Woodburn
P O Box 9570
Amarillo TX 79105-9570
806/379-2300

Presidio County
Brenda M. Silva
P O Box 789
Marfa TX 79843
915/729-4812

Rains County
Mary Sheppard
P O Box 187
Emory TX 75440-0187
903/473-2461

Randall County
Jo Carter
P O Box 1096
Canyon TX 79015-1096
806/655-6200

Reagan County
Terri Pullig
P O Box 100
Big Lake TX 76932
915/884-2442

Real County
Bella A. Rubio
P O Box 750
Leakey TX 78873
830/232-5202

Red River County
Clara Gaddis
1007 E Main St
Clarksville TX 75426
903/427-3761

Reeves County
Pat Tarin
P O Box 848
Pecos TX 79772-0848
915/445-2714

Refugio County
Ruby Garcia
P O Box 736
Refugio TX 78377
361/526-2721

Roberts County
Donna L. Goodman
P O Box 477
Miami TX 79059-0477
806/868-2341

Robertson County
Cornelia A. Starkey
P O Box 250
Franklin TX 77856-0250
979/828-3636

Rockwall County
Kay McDaniel
1101 Ridge Rd, Ste 209
Rockwall TX 75087
972/882-0260

Runnels County
Loretta Michalewicz
P O Box 166
Ballinger TX 76821-0166
915/365-2638

Rusk County
Linda J. Smith
P O Box 1687
Henderson TX 75653
903/657-0353

Sabine County
Tanya Walker
P O Box 850
Hemphill TX 75948
409/787-2912

San Augustine County
Jean Steptoe
Co Courthouse, Rm 202
San Augustine TX 75972
936/275-2231

San Jacinto County
Marilyn Nettles
P O Box 369
Coldspring TX 77331
936/653-2909

San Patricio County
Patricia Norton
P O Box 1084
Sinton TX 78387-1084
361/364-6225

San Saba County
Kim Wells
500 E Wallace St, Rm 202
San Saba TX 76877
915/372-3375

Schleicher County
Peggy Williams
P O Box 580
Eldorado TX 76936-0580
915/853-2833

Scurry County
Trina Rodgers
1806 25th St, Ste 402
Snyder TX 79549
915/573-5641

Shackelford County
Cheri Hawkins
P O Box 247
Albany TX 76430-0247
915/762-2232

Shelby County
Marsha Singletary
P O Drawer 1953
Center TX 75935-1953
936/598-4164

Sherman County
Mary Lou Albert
P O Box 270
Stratford TX 79084
806/396-2371

Smith County
Becky Dempsey
100 N Broadway, Rm 204
Tyler TX 75702-7236
903/535-0666

Somervell County
Lovella Williams
P O Box 1098
Glen Rose TX 76043
254/897-4427

Starr County
Juan Erasmo Saenz
Co Courthouse, Rm 303
Rio Grande City TX 78582
956/487-2610

Stephens County
Shirley Parker
Co Courthouse, 2nd Fl
Breckenridge TX 76424
254/559-3151

Sterling County
Diane A. Haar
P O Box 55
Sterling City TX 76951
915/378-5191

Stonewall County
Betty L. Smith
P O Drawer P
Aspermont TX 79502
940/989-2272

Sutton County
Veronica E. Hernandez
300 E Oak, Ste 3
Sonora TX 76950
915/387-3815

Swisher County
Brenda Hudson
Co Courthouse
Tulia TX 79088-2297
806/995-4396

Tarrant County
Thomas A. Wilder
401 W Belknap
Fort Worth TX 76196
817/884-1574

Taylor County
Patricia Henderson
300 Oak St
Abilene TX 79602-1580
915/674-1316

Terrell County
Martha Allen
P O Drawer 410
Sanderson TX 79848
915/345-2391

Terry County
Paige Lindsey
500 W Main, Rm 209E
Brownfield TX 79316
806/637-4202

Throckmorton County
Melanie Jones
P O Box 309
Throckmorton TX 76483
940/849-2501

Titus County
Bobby LaPrade
P O Box 492
Mount Pleasant TX 75456
903/577-6724

Tom Green County
Sheri Woodfin
112 W Beauregard
San Angelo TX 76903
915/659-6579

Travis County
Amalia Rodriguez-
Mendoza
P O Box 1748
Austin TX 78767-1748
512/473-9457

Trinity County
Cheryl Cartwright
P O Box 548
Groveton TX 75845-0548
936/642-1118

Tyler County
Melissie Evans
100 W Bluff, 203
Courthouse
Woodville TX 75979-5220
409/283-2162

Upshur County
Frankie M. Hamberlin
P O Box 950
Gilmer TX 75644
903/843-5031

Upton County
Phyllis Stephens
P O Box 465
Rankin TX 79778
915/693-2861

Uvalde County
Lydia Steele
Co Courthouse, No 15
Uvalde TX 78801-5299
830/278-3918

Val Verde County
Martha Mitchell
P O Box 1544
Del Rio TX 78841-1544
830/774-7538

Van Zandt County
Nancy Young
121 E Dallas, Rm 302
Canton TX 75103-1604
903/567-6576

Victoria County
Mary Elizabeth Jimenez
P O Box 2238
Victoria TX 77902-2238
361/575-0581

Walker County
Bernice Coleman
1100 University Ave, #301
Huntsville TX 77340
936/436-4972

Waller County
Pat Spadachene
836 Austin St, Rm 318
Hempstead TX 77445
979/826-7735

Ward County
Pam Bingham
P O Box 440
Monahans TX 79756
915/943-2751

Washington County
Vicki Lehmann
100 E Main, Ste 304
Brenham TX 77833-3753
979/277-6200

Webb County
Manuel Gutierrez
1110 Victoria, Ste 202
Laredo TX 78042
956/721-2460

Wharton County
Denice K. Malota
P O Drawer 391
Wharton TX 77488-0391
979/532-5542

Wheeler County
Sherri Jones
P O Box 528
Wheeler TX 79096-0528
806/826-5931

Wichita County
Dorsey R. Trapp
P O Box 718
Wichita Falls TX 76307
940/766-8190

Wilbarger County
Wilda Byers
1700 Wilbarger St, Rm 33
Vernon TX 76384-4749
940/553-3411

Willacy County
S. V. (Chago) Fonseca
Co Courthouse, 2nd Fl
Raymondville TX 78580
956/689-2532

Williamson County
Bonnie Wolbrueck
P O Box 24
Georgetown TX 78627
512/943-1212

Wilson County
Shirley Polasek
P O Box 812
Floresville TX 78114
830/393-7322

Winkler County
Sherry Terry
P O Box 1065
Kermit TX 79745-1065
915/586-3359

Wise County
Lawana Snider
P O Box 308
Decatur TX 76234
940/627-5535

Wood County
Novis Wisdom
P O Box 1707
Quitman TX 75783-1707
903/763-2361

Yoakum County
Vicki Blundell
P O Box 899
Plains TX 79355-0899
806/456-7453

Young County
Carolyn Collins
516 4th St, Rm 201
Graham TX 76450-2964
940/549-0029

Zapata County
Consuelo R. Villarreal
P O Box 788
Zapata TX 78076-0788
956/765-9930

Zavala County
Frankie G. Mancha
P O Box 704
Crystal City TX 78839-0704
830/374-3456

APPENDIX C

TEXAS
FAMILY CODE

(RELEVANT PORTIONS)

CHAPTER 3. MARITAL PROPERTY RIGHTS AND LIABILITIES

SUBCHAPTER A. GENERAL RULES FOR SEPARATE AND COMMUNITY PROPERTY

§ 3.001. Separate Property

A spouse's separate property consists of:

(1) the property owned or claimed by the spouse before marriage;

(2) the property acquired by the spouse during marriage by gift, devise, or descent; and

(3) the recovery for personal injuries sustained by the spouse during marriage, except any recovery for loss of earning capacity during marriage.

§ 3.002. Community Property

Community property consists of the property, other than separate property, acquired by either spouse during marriage.

§ 3.003. Presumption of Community Property

(a) Property possessed by either spouse during or on dissolution of marriage is presumed to be community property.

SUBCHAPTER C. MARITAL PROPERTY LIABILITIES

§ 3.201. Spousal Liability

(a) A person is personally liable for the acts of the person's spouse only if:

(1) the spouse acts as an agent *for* the person; or

(2) the spouse incurs a debt for necessaries as provided by Subchapter F, Chapter 2.

(b) Except as provided by this subchapter, community property is not subject to a liability that arises from an act of a spouse.

(c) A spouse does not act as an agent for the other spouse solely because of the marriage relationship.

SUBCHAPTER A. GROUNDS FOR DIVORCE AND DEFENSES

§ 6.001. Insupportability

On the petition of either party to a marriage, the court may grant a divorce without regard to fault if the marriage has become insupportable because of discord or conflict of personalities that destroys the legitimate ends of the marital relationship and prevents any reasonable expectation of reconciliation.

SUBCHAPTER D. JURISDICTION, VENUE, AND RESIDENCE QUALIFICATIONS

§ 6.301. General Residency Rule for Divorce Suit

A suit for divorce may not be maintained in this state unless at the time the suit is filed either the petitioner or the respondent has been:

(1) a domiciliary of this state for the preceding six-month period; and

(2) a resident of the county in which the suit is filed for the preceding 90-day period.

§ 6.302. Suit for Divorce by Nonresident Spouse

If one spouse has been a domiciliary of this state for at least the last six months, a spouse domiciled in another state or nation may file a suit for divorce in the county in which the domiciliary spouse resides at the time the petition is filed.

§ 6.4035. Waiver of Service

(a) A party to a suit for the dissolution of a marriage may waive the issuance or service of process after the suit is filed by filing with the clerk of the court in which the suit is filed the waiver of the party acknowledging receipt of a copy of the filed petition.

(b) The waiver must contain the mailing address of the party who executed the waiver.

(c) The waiver must be sworn but may not be sworn before an attorney in the suit.

§ 6.404. Statement on Alternate Dispute Resolution

(a) A party to a proceeding under this title shall include in the first pleading filed by the party in the proceeding the following statement:

"I AM AWARE THAT IT IS THE POLICY OF THE STATE OF TEXAS TO PROMOTE THE AMICABLE AND NONJUDICIAL SETTLEMENT OF DISPUTES INVOLVING CHILDREN AND FAMILIES. I AM AWARE OF ALTERNATIVE DISPUTE RESOLUTION METHODS, INCLUDING MEDIATION. WHILE I RECOGNIZE THAT ALTERNATIVE DISPUTE RESOLUTION IS AN ALTERNATIVE TO AND NOT A SUBSTITUTE FOR A TRIAL AND THAT THIS CASE MAY BE TRIED IF IT IS NOT SETTLED, I REPRESENT TO THE COURT THAT I WILL ATTEMPT IN GOOD FAITH TO RESOLVE BEFORE FINAL TRIAL CONTESTED ISSUES IN THIS CASE BY ALTERNATIVE DISPUTE RESOLUTION WITHOUT THE NECESSITY OF COURT INTERVENTION."

(b) The statement prescribed by Subsection (a) must be prominently displayed in boldfaced type or capital letters or be underlined and be signed by the party.

§ 6.405. Protective Order

(a) The petition in a suit for dissolution of a marriage must state whether a protective order under Title 4 is in effect or if an application for a protective order is pending with regard to the parties to the suit.

(b) The petitioner shall attach to the petition a copy of each protective order issued under Title 4 in which one of the parties to the suit was the applicant and the other party was the respondent without regard to the date of the order. If a copy of the protective order is not available at the time of filing, the petition must state that a copy of the order will be filed with the court before any hearing.

§ 6.406. Mandatory Joinder of Suit Affecting Parent-Child Relationship

(a) The petition in a suit for dissolution of a marriage shall state whether there are children born or adopted of the marriage who are under 18 years of age or who are otherwise entitled to support as provided by Chapter *154*.

(b) If the parties are parents of a child, as defined by Section 101.003, and the child is not under the continuing jurisdiction of another court as provided by Chapter *155*, the suit for dissolution of a marriage must include a suit affecting the parent-child relationship under Title *5*.

§ 6.702. Waiting Period

(a) The court may not grant a divorce before the 60th day after the date the suit was filed. A decree rendered in violation of this subsection is not subject to collateral attack.

§ 6.710. Copy of Decree

The clerk of the court shall mail a copy of the final decree of dissolution of a marriage to the party who waived service of process under Section 6.4035 by mailing the copy of the decree to the party at the mailing address contained in the waiver or to the office of the party's attorney of record.

§ 7.001. General Rule of Property Division

In a decree of divorce or annulment, the court shall order a division of the estate of the parties in a manner that the court deems just and right, having due regard for the rights of each party and any children of the marriage.

CHAPTER 8. MAINTENANCE

§ 8.001. Definition

In this chapter, "maintenance" means an award in a suit for dissolution of a marriage of periodic payments from the future income of one spouse for the support of the other spouse.

§ 8.002. Eligibility for Maintenance; Court Order

(a) In a suit for dissolution of a marriage or in a proceeding for maintenance in a court with personal jurisdiction over both former spouses following the dissolution of their marriage by a court that lacked personal jurisdiction over an absent spouse, the court may order maintenance for either spouse only if:

(1) the spouse from whom maintenance is requested was convicted of or received deferred adjudication for a criminal offense that also constitutes an act of family violence under Title 4 and the offense occurred:

(A) within two years before the date on which a suit for dissolution of the marriage is filed; or

(B) while the suit is pending; or

(2) the duration of the marriage was 10 years or longer, the spouse seeking maintenance lacks sufficient property, including property distributed to the spouse under this code, to provide for

the spouse's minimum reasonable needs, as limited by Section 8.005, and the spouse seeking maintenance:

(A) is unable to support himself or herself through appropriate employment because of an incapacitating physical or mental disability;

(B) is the custodian of a child who requires substantial care and personal supervision because a physical or mental disability makes it necessary, taking into consideration the needs of the child, that the spouse not be employed outside the home; or

(C) clearly lacks earning ability in the labor market adequate to provide support for the spouse's minimum reasonable needs, as limited by Section 8.005.

(b) A court may enforce an order for spousal maintenance under this section by ordering garnishment of the wages of the person ordered to pay the maintenance or by any other means available under Section 8.009.

§ 8.003. Factors in Determining Maintenance

A court that determines that a spouse is eligible to receive maintenance under this chapter shall determine the nature, amount, duration, and manner of periodic payments by considering all relevant factors, including:

(1) the financial resources of the spouse seeking maintenance, including the community and separate property and liabilities apportioned to that spouse in the dissolution proceeding, and that spouse's ability to meet the spouse's needs independently;

(2) the education and employment skills of the spouses, the time necessary to acquire sufficient education or training to enable the spouse seeking maintenance to find appropriate employment, the availability of that education or training, and the feasibility of that education or training;

(3) the duration of the marriage;

(4) the age, employment history, earning ability, and physical and emotional condition of the spouse seeking maintenance;

(5) the ability of the spouse from whom maintenance is requested to meet that spouse's personal needs and to provide periodic child support payments, if applicable, while meeting the personal needs of the spouse seeking maintenance;

(6) acts by either spouse resulting in excessive or abnormal expenditures or destruction, concealment, or fraudulent disposition of community property, joint tenancy, or other property

held in common;

(7) the comparative financial resources of the spouses, including medical, retirement, insurance, or other benefits, and the separate property of each spouse;

(8) the contribution by one spouse to the education, training, or increased earning power of the other spouse;

(9) the property brought to the marriage by either spouse;

(10) the contribution of a spouse as homemaker;

(11) marital misconduct of the spouse seeking maintenance; and

(12) the efforts of the spouse seeking maintenance to pursue available employment counseling as provided by Chapter 304, Labor Code.

§ 8.004. Presumption

(a) Except as provided by Subsection (b), it is presumed that maintenance is not warranted unless the spouse seeking maintenance has exercised diligence in:

(1) seeking suitable employment; or

(2) developing the necessary skills to become self-supporting during a period of separation and during the time the suit for dissolution of the marriage is pending.

(b) This section does not apply to a spouse who is not able to satisfy the presumption in Subsection (a) because of an incapacitating physical or mental disability.

§ 8.005. Duration of Maintenance Order

(a) Except as provided by Subsection (b), a court:

(1) may not order maintenance that remains in effect for more than three years after the date of the order; and

(2) shall limit the duration of a maintenance order to the shortest reasonable period that allows the spouse seeking maintenance to meet the spouse's minimum reasonable needs by obtaining appropriate employment or developing an appropriate skill, unless the ability of the spouse to provide for the spouse's minimum reasonable needs through employment is substantially or totally diminished because of:

(A) physical or mental disability;

(B) duties as the custodian of an infant or young child; or

(C) another compelling impediment to gainful employment.

(b) If a spouse seeking maintenance is unable to support himself or herself through appropriate employment because of an incapacitating physical or mental disability, the court may order maintenance for an indefinite period for as long as the disability continues. The court may order periodic review of its order, on the request of either party or on its own motion, to determine whether the disability is continuing. The continuation of spousal maintenance under these circumstances is subject to a motion to modify as provided by Section 8.008.

§ 8.006. Amount of Maintenance

(a) A court may not order maintenance that requires a spouse to pay monthly more than the lesser of:

(1) $2,500; or

(2) 20 percent of the spouse's average monthly gross income.

(b) The court shall set the amount that a spouse is required to pay in a maintenance order to provide for the minimum reasonable needs of the spouse receiving the maintenance under the order, considering employment or property received in the dissolution of the marriage or otherwise owned by the spouse receiving the maintenance that contributes to the minimum reasonable needs of that spouse.

(c) Department of Veterans Affairs service-connected disability compensation, social security benefits and disability benefits, and workers' compensation benefits are excluded from maintenance.

§ 8.007. Termination

(a) The obligation to pay future maintenance terminates on the death of either party or on the

remarriage of the party receiving maintenance.

(b) After a hearing, the court shall terminate the maintenance order if the party receiving maintenance cohabits with another person in a permanent place of abode on a continuing, conjugal basis.

§ 153.001. Public Policy

(a) The public policy of this state is to:

(1) assure that children will have frequent and continuing contact with parents who have shown the ability to act in the best interest of the child;

(2) provide a safe, stable, and nonviolent environment for the child; and

(3) encourage parents to share in the rights and duties of raising their child after the parents have separated or dissolved their marriage.

(b) A court may not render an order that conditions the right of a conservator to possession of or access to a child on the payment of child support.

§ 153.003. No Discrimination Based on Sex or Marital Status

The court shall consider the qualifications of the parties without regard to their marital status or to the sex of the party or the child in determining:

(1) which party to appoint as sole managing conservator;

(2) whether to appoint a party as joint managing conservator; and

(3) the terms and conditions of conservatorship and possession of and access to the child.

§ 153.007. Agreement Concerning Conservatorship

(a) To promote the amicable settlement of disputes between the parties to a suit, the parties may enter into a written agreement containing provisions for conservatorship and possession of the child and for modification of the agreement, including variations from the standard possession order.

(b) If the court finds that the agreement is in the child's best interest, the court shall render an order in accordance with the agreement.

(c) Terms of the agreement contained in the order or incorporated by reference regarding conservatorship or support of or access to a child in an order may be enforced by all remedies available for enforcement of a judgment, including contempt, but are not enforceable as a contract.

(d) If the court finds the agreement is not in the child's best interest, the court may request the parties to submit a revised agreement or the court may render an order for the conservatorship and possession of the child.

§ 153.073. Rights of Parent at All Times

(a) Unless limited by court order, a parent appointed as a conservator of a child has at all times the right:

(1) as specified by court order:

(A) to receive information from the other parent concerning the health, education, and welfare of the child; and

(B) to confer with the other parent to the extent possible before making a decision concerning the health, education, and welfare of the child;

(2) of access to medical, dental, psychological, and educational records of the child;

(3) to consult with a physician, dentist, or psychologist of the child;

(4) to consult with school officials concerning the child's welfare and educational status, including school activities;

(5) to attend school activities;

(6) to be designated on the child's records as a person to be notified in case of an emergency;

(7) to consent to medical, dental, and surgical treatment during an emergency involving an immediate danger to the health and safety of the child; and

(8) to manage the estate of the child to the extent the estate has been created by the parent or the parent's family.

(b) The court shall specify in the order the rights that a parent retains at all times.

§ 153.074. Rights and Duties During Period of Possession

Unless limited by court order, a parent appointed as a conservator of a child has the following rights and duties during the period that the parent has possession of the child:

(1) the duty of care, control, protection, and reasonable discipline of the child;

(2) the duty to support the child, including providing the child with clothing, food, shelter, and medical and dental care not involving an invasive procedure;

(3) the right to consent for the child to medical and dental care not involving an invasive procedure;

(4) the right to consent for the child to medical, dental, and surgical treatment during an emergency involving immediate danger to the health and safety of the child; and

(5) the right to direct the moral and religious training of the child.;

§ 153.076. Parents' Duty to Provide Information

(a) If both parents are appointed as conservators of the child, the court shall order that each parent has a duty to inform the other parent in a timely manner of significant information concerning the health, education, and welfare of the child.

(b) If both parents are appointed as conservators of a child, the court shall order that each parent has the duty to inform the other parent if the parent resides with for at least 30 days, marries, or intends to marry a person who the parent knows:

(1) is registered as a sex offender under Chapter 62, Code of Criminal Procedure, as added by Chapter 668, Acts of the 75th Legislature, Regular Session, 1997; or

(2) is currently charged with an offense for which on conviction the person would be required to register under that chapter.

(c) The notice required to be made under Subsection (b) must be made as soon as practicable but not later than the 40th day after the date the parent begins to reside with the person or the 10th day after the date the marriage occurs, as appropriate. The notice must include a description of the offense that is the basis of the person's requirement to register as a sex offender or of the offense with which the person is charged.

(d) A person commits an offense if the person fails to provide notice in the manner required by Subsections (b) and (c). An offense under this subsection is a Class C misdemeanor.

§ 153.131. Presumption That Parent to be Appointed Managing Conservator

(a) Subject to the prohibition in Section 153.004, unless the court finds that appointment of the parent or parents would not be in the best interest of the child because the appointment would significantly impair the child's physical health or emotional development, a parent shall be appointed sole managing conservator or both parents shall be appointed as joint managing conservators of the child.

(b) It is a rebuttable presumption that the appointment of the parents of a child as joint managing conservators is in the best interest of the child. A finding of a history of family violence involving the parents of a child removes the presumption under this subsection.

§ 153.133. Agreement for Joint Managing Conservatorship

(a) If a written agreement of the parents is filed with the court, the court shall render an order appointing the parents as joint managing conservators only if the agreement:

(1) designates the conservator who has the exclusive right to establish the primary residence of the child and:

(A) establishes, until modified by further order, the geographic area within which the conservator shall maintain the child's primary residence; or

(B) specifies that the conservator may establish the child's primary residence without regard to geographic location;

(2) specifies the rights and duties of each parent regarding the child's physical care, support, and education;

(3) includes provisions to minimize disruption of the child's education, daily routine, and association with friends;

(4) allocates between the parents, independently, jointly, or exclusively, all of the remaining rights and duties of a parent provided by Chapter 151;

(5) is voluntarily and knowingly made by each parent and has not been repudiated by either parent at the time the order is rendered; and

(6) is in the best interest of the child.

(b) The agreement may contain an alternative dispute resolution procedure that the parties agree to use before requesting enforcement or modification of the terms and conditions of the joint conservatorship through litigation, except in an emergency.

§ 153.135. Equal Possession Not Required

Joint managing conservatorship does not require the award of equal or nearly equal periods of
physical possession of and access to the child to each of the joint conservators.

§ 153.136. Court Designation of Primary Physical Residence

If joint managing conservatorship is ordered, the best interest of the child ordinarily requires the court to designate a primary physical residence for the child.

§ 153.137. Guidelines for the Possession of Child by Parent Named as Joint Managing Conservator

The standard possession order provided by Subchapter F constitutes a presumptive minimum amount of time for possession of a child by a parent named as a joint managing conservator who is not awarded the primary physical residence of the child in a suit.

§ 153.252. Rebuttable Presumption

In a suit, there is a rebuttable presumption that the standard possession order in Subchapter F:

(1) provides reasonable minimum possession of a child for a parent named as a possessory

conservator or joint managing conservator; and

(2) is in the best interest of the child.

SUBCHAPTER F. STANDARD POSSESSION ORDER

§ 153.311. Mutual Agreement or Specified Terms for Possession

The court shall specify in a standard possession order that the parties may have possession of the child at times mutually agreed to in advance by the parties and, in the absence of mutual agreement, shall have possession of the child under the specified terms set out in the standard order.

§ 153.312. Parents Who Reside 100 Miles or Less Apart

(a) If the possessory conservator resides 100 miles or less from the primary residence of the child, the possessory conservator shall have the right to possession of the child as follows:

(1) on weekends beginning at 6 p.m. on the first, third, and fifth Friday of each month and ending at 6 p.m. on the following Sunday or, at the possessory conservator's election made before or at the time of the rendition of the original or modification order, and as specified in the original or modification order, beginning at the time the child's school is regularly dismissed and ending at 6 p.m. on the following Sunday; and

(2) on Wednesdays of each week during the regular school term beginning at 6 p.m. and ending at 8 p.m., or, at the possessory conservator's election made before or at the time of the rendition of the original or modification order, and as specified in the original or modification order, beginning at the time the child's school is regularly dismissed and ending at the time the child's school resumes, unless the court finds that visitation under this subdivision is not in the best interest of the child.

(b) The following provisions govern possession of the child for vacations and certain specific holidays and supersede conflicting weekend or Wednesday periods of possession. The possessory conservator and the managing conservator shall have rights of possession of the child as follows:

(1) the possessory conservator shall have possession in even-numbered years, beginning at 6 p.m. on the day the child is dismissed from school for the school's spring vacation and ending at 6 p.m. on the day before school resumes after that vacation, and the managing conservator shall have possession for the same period in odd-numbered years;

(2) if a possessory conservator:

(A) gives the managing conservator written notice by April 1 of each year specifying an extended period or periods of summer possession, the possessory conservator shall have possession of the child for 30 days beginning not earlier than the day after the child's school is dismissed for the summer vacation and ending not later than seven days before school resumes at the end of the summer vacation, to be exercised in not more than two separate periods of at least seven consecutive days each; or

(B) does not give the managing conservator written notice by April 1 of each year specifying an extended period or periods of summer possession, the possessory conservator shall have possession of the child for 30 consecutive days beginning at 6 p.m. on July 1 and ending at 6 p.m. on July 31;

(3) if the managing conservator gives the possessory conservator written notice by April 15 of each year, the managing conservator shall have possession of the child on any one weekend beginning Friday at 6 p.m. and ending at 6 p.m. on the following Sunday during one period of possession by the possessory conservator under Subdivision (2), provided that the managing conservator picks up the child from the possessory conservator and returns the child to that same place; and

(4) if the managing conservator gives the possessory conservator written notice by April 15 of each year or gives the possessory conservator 14 days' written notice on or after April 16 of each year, the managing conservator may designate one weekend beginning not earlier than the day after the child's school is dismissed for the summer vacation and ending not later than seven days before school resumes at the end of the summer vacation, during which an otherwise scheduled weekend period of possession by the possessory conservator will not take place, provided that the weekend designated does not interfere with the possessory conservator's period or periods of extended summer possession or with Father's Day if the possessory conservator is the father of the child.

§ 153.313. Parents Who Reside Over 100 Miles Apart

If the possessory conservator resides more than 100 miles from the residence of the child, the possessory conservator shall have the right to possession of the child as follows:

(1) either regular weekend possession beginning on the first, third, and fifth Friday as provided under the terms applicable to parents who reside 100 miles or less apart or not more than one weekend per month of the possessory conservator's choice beginning at 6 p.m. on the day school recesses for the weekend and ending at 6 p.m. on the day before school resumes after the weekend, provided that the possessory conservator gives the managing conservator 14 days' written or telephonic notice preceding a designated weekend, and provided that the possessory conservator elects an option for this alternative period of possession by written notice given to the managing conservator within 90 days after the parties begin to reside more than 100 miles apart, as applicable;

(2) each year beginning on the day the child is dismissed from school for the school's spring vacation and ending at 6 p.m. on the day before school resumes after that vacation;

(3) if the possessory conservator:

(A) gives the managing conservator written notice by April 1 of each year specifying an extended period or periods of summer possession, the possessory conservator shall have possession of the child for 42 days beginning not earlier than the day after the child's school is dismissed for the summer vacation and ending not later than seven days before school resumes at the end of the summer vacation, to be exercised in not more than two separate periods of at least seven consecutive days each; or

(B) does not give the managing conservator written notice by April 1 of each year specifying an extended period or periods of summer possession, the possessory conservator shall have possession of the child for 42 consecutive days beginning at 6 p.m. on June 15 and ending at 6 p.m. on July 27;

(4) if the managing conservator gives the possessory conservator written notice by April 15 of each year the managing conservator shall have possession of the child on one weekend beginning Friday at 6 p.m. and ending at 6 p.m. on the following Sunday during one period of possession by the possessory conservator under Subdivision (3), provided that if a period of possession by the possessory conservator exceeds 30 days, the managing conservator may have possession of the child under the terms of this subdivision on two nonconsecutive weekends during that time period, and further provided that the managing conservator picks up the child from the possessory conservator and returns the child to that same place; and

(5) if the managing conservator gives the possessory conservator written notice by April 15 of each year, the managing conservator may designate 21 days beginning not earlier than the day after the child's school is dismissed for the summer vacation and ending not later than seven days before school resumes at the end of the summer vacation, to be exercised in not more than two separate periods of at least seven consecutive days each, during which the possessory conservator may not have possession of the child, provided that the period or periods so designated do not interfere with the possessory conservator's period or periods of extended summer possession or with Father's Day if the possessory conservator is the father of the child.

§ 153.314. Holiday Possession Unaffected by Distance Parents Reside Apart

The following provisions govern possession of the child for certain specific holidays and supersede conflicting weekend or Wednesday periods of possession without regard to the distance the parents reside apart. The possessory conservator and the managing conservator shall have rights of possession of the child as follows:

(1) the possessory conservator shall have possession of the child in even-numbered years beginning at 6 p.m. on the day the child is dismissed from school for the Christmas school vacation and ending at noon on December 26, and the managing conservator shall have possession for the same period in odd-numbered years;

(2) the possessory conservator shall have possession of the child in odd-numbered years beginning at noon on December 26 and ending at 6 p.m. on the day before school resumes after

that vacation, and the managing conservator shall have possession for the same period in even-numbered years;

(3) the possessory conservator shall have possession of the child in odd-numbered years, beginning at 6 p.m. on the day the child is dismissed from school before Thanksgiving and ending at 6 p.m. on the following Sunday, and the managing conservator shall have possession for the same period in even-numbered years;

(4) the parent not otherwise entitled under this standard order to present possession of a child on the child's birthday shall have possession of the child beginning at 6 p.m. and ending at 8 p.m. on that day, provided that the parent picks up the child from the residence of the conservator entitled to possession and returns the child to that same place;

(5) if a conservator, the father shall have possession of the child beginning at 6 p.m. on the Friday preceding Father's Day and ending on Father's Day at 6 p.m., provided that, if he is not otherwise entitled under this standard order to present possession of the child, he picks up the child from the residence of the conservator entitled to possession and returns the child to that same place; and

(6) if a conservator, the mother shall have possession of the child beginning at 6 p.m. on the Friday preceding Mother's Day and ending on Mother's Day at 6 p.m., provided that, if she is not otherwise entitled under this standard order to present possession of the child, she picks up the child from the residence of the conservator entitled to possession and returns the child to that same place.

§ 153.315. Weekend Possession Extended by Holiday

(a) If a weekend period of possession of the possessory conservator coincides with a school holiday during the regular school term or with a federal, state, or local holiday during the summer months in which school is not in session, the weekend possession shall end at 6 p.m. on a Monday holiday or school holiday or shall begin at 6 p.m. Thursday for a Friday holiday or school holiday, as applicable.

(b) At the possessory conservator's election, made before or at the time of the rendition of the original or modification order, and as specified in the original or modification order, periods of possession extended by a holiday may begin at the time the child's school is regularly dismissed.

§ 153.316. General Terms and Conditions

The court shall order the following general terms and conditions of possession of a child to apply without regard to the distance between the residence of a parent and the child:

(1) the managing conservator shall surrender the child to the possessory conservator at the beginning of each period of the possessory conservator's possession at the residence of the

managing conservator;

(2) if the possessory conservator elects to begin a period of possession at the time the child's school is regularly dismissed, the managing conservator shall surrender the child to the possessory conservator at the beginning of each period of possession at the school in which the child is enrolled;

(3) the possessory conservator shall be ordered to do one of the following:

(A) the possessory conservator shall surrender the child to the managing conservator at the end of each period of possession at the residence of the possessory conservator; or

(B) the possessory conservator shall return the child to the residence of the managing conservator at the end of each period of possession, except that the order shall provide that the possessory conservator shall surrender the child to the managing conservator at the end of each period of possession at the residence of the possessory conservator if:

(i) at the time the original order or a modification of an order establishing terms and conditions of possession or access the possessory conservator and the managing conservator lived in the same county, the possessory conservator's county of residence remains the same after the rendition of the order, and the managing conservator's county of residence changes, effective on the date of the change of residence by the managing conservator; or

(ii) the possessory conservator and managing conservator lived in the same residence at any time during a six-month period preceding the date on which a suit for dissolution of the marriage was filed and the possessory conservator's county of residence remains the same and the managing conservator's county of residence changes after they no longer live in the same residence, effective on the date the order is rendered;

(4) if the possessory conservator elects to end a period of possession at the time the child's school resumes, the possessory conservator shall surrender the child to the managing conservator at the end of each period of possession at the school in which the child is enrolled;

(5) each conservator shall return with the child the personal effects that the child brought at the beginning of the period of possession;

(6) either parent may designate a competent adult to pick up and return the child, as applicable; a parent or a designated competent adult shall be present when the child is picked up or returned;

(7) a parent shall give notice to the person in possession of the child on each occasion that the parent will be unable to exercise that parent's right of possession for a specified period;

(8) written notice shall be deemed to have been timely made if received or postmarked before or at the time that notice is due; and

(9) if a conservator's time of possession of a child ends at the time school resumes and for any reason the child is not or will not be returned to school, the conservator in possession of the child shall immediately notify the school and the other conservator that the child will not be or has not been returned to school.

§ 153.317. Alternative Possession Times

If a child is enrolled in school and the possessory conservator elects before or at the time of the rendition of the original or modification order, the standard order must expressly provide that the possessory conservator's period of possession shall begin or end, or both, at a different time expressly set in the standard order under and within the range of alternative times provided by one or both of the following subdivisions:

(1) instead of a period of possession by a possessory conservator beginning at 6 p.m. on the day school recesses, the period of possession may be set in the standard possession order to begin at the time the child's school is regularly dismissed or at any time between the time the child's school is regularly dismissed and 6 p.m.; and

(2) except for Wednesday evening possession, instead of a period of possession by a possessory conservator ending at 6 p.m. on the day before school resumes, the period of possession may be set in the standard order to end at the time school resumes.

§ 154.001. Support of Child

(a) The court may order either or both parents to support a child in the manner specified by the order:

(1) until the child is 18 years of age or until graduation from high school, whichever occurs later;

(2) until the child is emancipated through marriage, through removal of the disabilities of minority by court order, or by other operation of law;

(3) until the death of the child; or

(4) if the child is disabled as defined in this chapter, for an indefinite period.

§ 154.002. Child Support Through High School Graduation

(a) If the child is fully enrolled in an accredited secondary school in a program leading toward a high school diploma or enrolled in courses for joint high school and junior college credit pursuant to Section 130.008, Education Code, the court may render an original support order or modify an existing order providing child support past the 18th birthday of the child.

(b) The request for a support order through high school graduation may be filed before or after the child's 18th birthday.

(c) The order for periodic support may provide that payments continue through the end of the month in which the child graduates.

§ 154.006. Termination of Duty of Support

(a) Unless otherwise agreed in writing or expressly provided in the order or as provided by Subsection (b), the child support order terminates on the marriage of the child, removal of the child's disabilities for general purposes, or death of the child or a parent ordered to pay child support.

§ 154.007. Order to Withhold Child Support From Income

(a) In a proceeding in which periodic payments of child support are ordered, modified, or enforced, the court or Title IV-D agency shall order that income be withheld from the disposable earnings of the obligor as provided by Chapter 158.

(b) If the court does not order income withholding, an order for support must contain a provision for income withholding to ensure that withholding may be effected if a delinquency occurs.

(c) A child support order must be construed to contain a withholding provision even if the provision has been omitted from the written order.

(d) If the order was rendered or last modified before January 1, 1987, the order is presumed to contain a provision for income withholding procedures to take effect in the event a delinquency occurs without further amendment to the order or future action by the court.

§ 154.008. Provision for Health Insurance Coverage

The court shall order health insurance coverage for the child as provided by Subchapters B and D.

§ 154.010. No Discrimination Based on Marital Status of Parents or Sex

The amount of support ordered for the benefit of a child shall be determined without regard to:

(1) the sex of the obligor, obligee, or child; or

(2) the marital status of the parents of the child.

§ 154.011. Support Not Conditioned on Possession or Access

A court may not render an order that conditions the payment of child support on whether a managing conservator allows a possessory conservator to have possession of or access to a child.

§ 154.061. Computing Net Monthly Income

(a) Whenever feasible, gross income should first be computed on an annual basis and then should be recalculated to determine average monthly gross income.

(b) The Title IV—D agency shall annually promulgate tax charts to compute net monthly income, subtracting from gross income social security taxes and federal income tax withholding for a single person claiming one personal exemption and the standard deduction.

§ 154.062. Net Resources

(a) The court shall calculate net resources for the purpose of determining child support liability as provided by this section.

(b) Resources include:

(1) 100 percent of all wage and salary income and other compensation for personal services (including commissions, overtime pay, tips, and bonuses);

(2) interest, dividends, and royalty income;

(3) self-employment income;

(4) net rental income (defined as rent after deducting operating expenses and mortgage payments, but not including noncash items such as depreciation); and

(5) all other income actually being received, including severance pay, retirement benefits, pensions, trust income, annuities, capital gains, social security benefits, unemployment benefits, disability and workers' compensation benefits, interest income from notes regardless of the source, gifts and prizes, spousal maintenance, and alimony.

(c) Resources do not include:

(1) return of principal or capital;

(2) accounts receivable; or

(3) benefits paid in accordance with aid for families with dependent children.

(d) The court shall deduct the following items from resources to determine the net resources available for child support:

(1) social security taxes;

(2) federal income tax based on the tax rate for a single person claiming one personal exemption and the standard deduction;

(3) state income tax;

(4) union dues; and

(5) expenses for health insurance coverage for the obligor's child.

§ 154.064. Health Insurance for Child Presumptively Provided by Obligor

The guidelines for support of a child are based on the assumption that the court will order the obligor to provide health insurance coverage for the child in addition to the amount of child support calculated in accordance with those guidelines.

§ 154.065. Self-Employment Income

(a) Income from self-employment, whether positive or negative, includes benefits allocated to an individual from a business or undertaking in the form of a proprietorship, partnership, joint venture, close corporation, agency, or independent contractor, less ordinary and necessary expenses required to produce that income.

(b) In its discretion, the court may exclude from self-employment income amounts allowable under federal income tax law as depreciation, tax credits, or any other business expenses shown by the evidence to be inappropriate in making the determination of income available for the purpose of calculating child support.

§ 154.12 1. Guidelines for the Support of a Child

The child support guidelines in this subchapter are intended to guide the court in determining an equitable amount of child support.

§ 154.122. Application of Guidelines Rebuttably Presumed in Best Interest of Child

(a) The amount of a periodic child support payment established by the child support guidelines in effect in this state at the time of the hearing is presumed to be reasonable, and an order of support conforming to the guidelines is presumed to be in the best interest of the child.

(b) A court may determine that the application of the guidelines would be unjust or inappropriate under the circumstances.

§ 154.123. Additional Factors for Court to Consider

(a) The court may order periodic child support payments in an amount other than that established by the guidelines if the evidence rebuts the presumption that application of the guidelines is in the best interest of the child and justifies a variance from the guidelines.

(b) In determining whether application of the guidelines would be unjust or inappropriate under the circumstances, the court shall consider evidence of all relevant factors, including:

(1) the age and needs of the child;

(2) the ability of the parents to contribute to the support of the child;

(3) any financial resources available for the support of the child;

(4) the amount of time of possession of and access to a child;

(5) the amount of the obligee's net resources, including the earning potential of the obligee if the actual income of the obligee is significantly less than what the obligee could earn because the obligee is intentionally unemployed or underemployed and including an increase or decrease in the income of the obligee or income that may be attributed to the property and assets of the obligee;

(6) child care expenses incurred by either party in order to maintain gainful employment;

(7) whether either party has the managing conservatorship or actual physical custody of another child;

(8) the amount of alimony or spousal maintenance actually and currently being paid or received by a party;

(9) the expenses for a son or daughter for education beyond secondary school;

(10) whether the obligor or obligee has an automobile, housing, or other benefits furnished by his or her employer, another person, or a business entity;

(11) the amount of other deductions from the wage or salary income and from other compensation for personal services of the parties;

(12) provision for health care insurance and payment of uninsured medical expenses;

(13) special or extraordinary educational, health care, or other expenses of the parties or of the child;

(14) the cost of travel in order to exercise possession of and access to a child;

(15) positive or negative cash flow from any real and personal property and assets, including a business and investments;

(16) debts or debt service assumed by either party; and

(17) any other reason consistent with the best interest of the child, taking into consideration the circumstances of the parents.

§ 154.124. Agreement Concerning Support

(a) To promote the amicable settlement of disputes between the parties to a suit, the parties may enter into a written agreement containing provisions for support of the child and for modification of the agreement, including variations from the child support guidelines provided by Subchapter C.

(b) If the court finds that the agreement is in the child's best interest, the court shall render an order in accordance with the agreement.

(c) Terms of the agreement in the order may be enforced by all remedies available for enforcement of a judgment, including contempt, but are not enforceable as contract terms unless provided by the agreement.

(d) If the court finds the agreement is not in the child's best interest, the court may request the parties to submit a revised agreement or the court may render an order for the support of the child.

§ 154.125. Application of Guidelines to Net Resources of $6,000 or Less

(a) The guidelines for the support of a child in this section are specifically designed to apply to situations in which the obligor's monthly net resources are $6,000 or less.

(b) If the obligor's monthly net resources are $6,000 or less, the court shall presumptively apply the following schedule in rendering the child support order:

CHILD SUPPORT GUIDELINES BASED ON THE MONTHLY NET RESOURCES OF THE OBLIGOR

1 child 20% of Obligor's Net Resources

2 children 25% of Obligor's Net Resources

3 children 30% of Obligor's Net Resources

4 children 35% of Obligor's Net Resources

5 children 40% of Obligor's Net Resources

6+ children Not less than the amount for 5 children

§ 154.126. Application of Guidelines to Net Resources of More Than $6,000 Monthly

(a) If the obligor's net resources exceed $6,000 per month, the court shall presumptively apply the percentage guidelines to the first $6,000 of the obligor's net resources. Without further reference to the percentage recommended by these guidelines, the court may order additional amounts of child support as appropriate, depending on the income of the parties and the proven needs of the child.

(b) The proper calculation of a child support order that exceeds the presumptive amount established for the first $6,000 of the obligor's net resources requires that the entire amount of the presumptive award be subtracted from the proven total needs of the child. After the presumptive award is subtracted, the court shall allocate between the parties the responsibility to meet the additional needs of the child according to the circumstances of the parties. However, in no event may the obligor be required to pay more child support than the greater of the presumptive amount or the amount equal to 100 percent of the proven needs of the child.

§ 154.127. Partial Termination of Support Obligation

A child support order for more than one child shall provide that, on the termination of support for a child, the level of support for the remaining child or children is in accordance with the child support guidelines.

§ 154.128. Computing Support for Children in More Than One Household

(a) In applying the child support guidelines for an obligor who has children in more than one household, the court shall apply the percentage guidelines in this subchapter by making the following computation:

(1) determine the amount of child support that would be ordered if all children whom the obligor has the legal duty to support lived in one household by applying the schedule in this subchapter;

(2) compute a child support credit for the obligor's children who are not before the court by dividing the amount determined under Subdivision (1) by the total number of children whom the obligor is obligated to support and multiplying that number by the number of the obligor's children who are not before the court;

(3) determine the adjusted net resources of the obligor by subtracting the child support credit computed under Subdivision (2) from the net resources of the obligor; and

(4) determine the child support amount for the children before the court by applying the percentage guidelines for one household for the number of children of the obligor before the court to the obligor's adjusted net resources.

(b) For the purpose of determining a child support credit, the total number of an obligor's children includes the children before the court for the establishment or modification of a support order and any other children, including children residing with the obligor, whom the obligor has the legal duty of support.

(c) The child support credit with respect to children for whom the obligor is obligated by an order to pay support is computed, regardless of whether the obligor is delinquent in child support payments, without regard to the amount of the order.

§ 154.129. Alternative Method of Computing Support for Children in More Than One Household

In lieu of performing the computation under the preceding section, the court may determine the child support amount for the children before the court by applying the percentages in the table below to the obligor's net resources:

MULTIPLE FAMILY ADJUSTED GUIDELINES
(% OF NET RESOURCES)
Number of Children Before the Court

		1	2	3	4	5	6	7
Number of	0	20.00	25.00	30.00	35.00	40.00	40.00	40.00
other	1	17.50	22.50	27.38	32.20	37.33	37.71	38.00
children for	2	16.00	20.63	25.20	30.33	35.43	36.00	36.44
whom the	3	14.75	19.00	24.00	29.00	34.00	34.67	35.20
obligor	4	13.60	18.33	23.14	28.00	32.89	33.60	34.18
has a	5	13.33	17.86	22.50	27.22	32.00	32.73	33.33
duty of	6	13.14	17.50	22.00	26.60	31.27	32.00	32.62
support	7	13.00	17.22	21.60	26.09	30.67	31.38	32.00

§ 154.181. Medical Support Order

In a suit affecting the parent-child relationship or in a proceeding under Chapter 159, the court shall render an order for the medical support of the child.

§ 154.182. Health Insurance

(a) The court shall consider the cost and quality of health insurance coverage available to the parties and shall give priority to health insurance coverage available through the employment of one of the parties.

(b) Except as provided for by Subdivision (6), in determining the manner in which health insurance for the child is to be ordered, the court shall render its order in accordance with the following priorities, unless a party shows good cause why a particular order would not be in the best interest of the child:

(1) if health insurance is available for the child through the obligor's employment or membership in a union, trade association, or other organization, the court shall order the obligor to include the child in the obligor's health insurance;

(2) if health insurance is not available for the child through the obligor's employment but is available for the child through the obligee's employment or membership in a union, trade association, or other organization, the court may order the obligee to provide health insurance for the child, and, in such event, shall order the obligor to pay additional child support to be withheld from earnings under Chapter 158 to the obligee for the actual cost of the health insurance for the child;

(3) if health insurance is not available for the child under Subdivision (1) or (2), the court shall order the obligor to provide health insurance for the child if the court finds that health insurance is available for the child from another source and that the obligor is financially able to provide it;

(4) if health insurance is not available for the child under Subdivision (1), (2), or (3), the court shall order the obligor to apply for coverage through the Texas Healthy Kids Corporation established under Chapter 109, Health and Safety Code;

(5) if health coverage is not available for the child under Subdivision (1), (2), (3), or (4), the court shall order the obligor to pay the obligee, in addition to any amount ordered under the guidelines for child support, a reasonable amount each month as medical support for the child to be withheld from earnings under Chapter 158; or

(6) notwithstanding Subdivisions (1) through (3), an obligor whose employer, union, trade association, or other organization does not offer a child/children coverage option in lieu of a spouse/child/children option of health insurance coverage may elect to apply for coverage through the Texas Healthy Kids Corporation. An obligor required to pay additional child support to an obligee for health insurance coverage may elect to apply for coverage through the Texas Healthy Kids Corporation if the obligee's employer, union, trade association, or other organization does not offer a child/children coverage option in lieu of a spouse/child/children option of health insurance coverage.

(c) In establishing the amount of additional medical child support under Subsection (b)(5), the court shall presume that $38 each month is a reasonable amount for a child but may order a greater or lesser amount as appropriate under the circumstances. The Health and Human Services Commission may promulgate guidelines for the dollar amounts of medical child support that the court may presumptively apply in circumstances in which the obligor is responsible for medical child support for more than one child.

§ 154.183. Health Insurance Additional Support Duty of Obligor

(a) An amount that an obligor is required to pay for health insurance for the child:

(1) is in addition to the amount that the obligor is required to pay for child support under the guidelines for child support;

(2) is a child support obligation; and

(3) may be enforced as a child support obligation.

(b) If the court finds and states in the child support order that the obligee will maintain health insurance coverage for the child at the obligee's expense, the court may increase the amount of child support to be paid by the obligor in an amount not exceeding the total expense to the obligee for maintaining health insurance coverage.

(c) As additional child support, the court shall allocate between the parties, according to their circumstances, the reasonable and necessary health care expenses of a child that are not reimbursed by health insurance.

§ 154.185. Parent to Furnish Information

(a) The court shall order a parent providing health insurance to furnish to either the obligee, obligor, local domestic relations office, or Title IV—D agency the following information not later than the 30th day after the date the notice of rendition of the order is received:

(1) the social security number of the parent;

(2) the name and address of the parent's employer;

(3) whether the employer is self-insured or has health insurance available;

(4) proof that health insurance has been provided for the child;

(5) if the employer has health insurance available, the name of the health insurance carrier, the number of the policy, a copy of the policy and schedule of benefits, a health insurance membership card, claim forms, and any other information necessary to submit a claim; and

(6) if the employer is self-insured, a copy of the schedule of benefits, a membership card, claim forms, and any other information necessary to submit a claim.

(b) The court shall also order a parent providing health insurance to furnish the obligor, obligee, local domestic relations office, or Title IV—D agency with additional information regarding health insurance coverage not later than the 15th day after the date the information is received by the parent.

§ 154.187. Duties of Employer

(a) An order or notice under this subchapter to an employer directing that health insurance coverage be provided to a child of an employee or member is binding on a current or subsequent employer on receipt without regard to the date the order was rendered. If the employee or member is eligible for dependent health coverage for the child, the employer shall immediately enroll the child in a health insurance plan regardless of whether the employee is enrolled in the plan. If dependent coverage is not available to the employee or member through the employer's health insurance plan or enrollment cannot be made permanent or if the employer is not responsible or otherwise liable for providing such coverage, the employer shall provide notice to the sender in accordance with Subsection (c).

(b) If additional premiums are incurred as a result of adding the child to the health insurance plan, the employer shall deduct the health insurance premium from the earnings of the employee in accordance with Chapter 158 and apply the amount withheld to payment of the insurance premium.

(c) An employer who has received an order or notice under this subchapter shall provide to the sender, by first class mail not later than the 30th day after the date the employer receives the order or notice, a statement that the child:

(1) has been enrolled in a health insurance plan; or

(2) cannot be enrolled or cannot be enrolled permanently in a health insurance plan and provide the reason why coverage or permanent coverage cannot be provided.

(d) If the employee ceases employment or if the health insurance coverage lapses, the employer shall provide to the sender, by first class mail not later than the 15th day after the date of the termination of employment or the lapse of the coverage, notice of the termination or lapse and of the availability of any conversion privileges.

(e) On request, the employer shall release to the sender information concerning the available health insurance coverage, including the name of the health insurance carrier, the policy number, a copy of the policy and schedule of benefits, a health insurance membership card, and claim forms.

(f) In this section, "sender" means the person sending the order under Section 154.186.

(g) An employer who fails to enroll a child, fails to withhold or remit premiums or cash medical support, or discriminates in hiring or employment on the basis of a medical support order shall be subject to the penalties and fines in Subchapter C, Chapter 158.

§ 154.188. Failure to Provide Required Health Insurance

A parent ordered to provide health insurance who fails to do so is liable for necessary medical expenses of the child, without regard to whether the expenses would have been paid if health insurance had been provided.

§ 154.189. Notice of Termination or Lapse of Insurance Coverage

(a) An obligor ordered to provide health insurance coverage for a child must notify the obligee and any child support agency enforcing a support obligation against the obligor of the:

(1) termination or lapse of health insurance coverage for the child not later than the 15th day after the date of a termination or lapse; and

(2) availability of additional health insurance to the obligor for the child after a termination or lapse of coverage not later than the 15th day after the date the insurance becomes available.

(b) If termination of coverage results from a change of employers, the obligor, the obligee, or the child support agency may send the new employer a copy of the order requiring the employee to provide health insurance for a child or notice of the medical support order as provided by this subchapter.

§ 154.190. Reenrolling Child for Insurance Coverage

After health insurance has been terminated or has lapsed, an obligor ordered to provide health insurance coverage for the child must enroll the child in a health insurance plan at the next available enrollment period.

§ 154.191. Remedy Not Exclusive

(a) This subchapter does not limit the rights of the obligor, obligee, local domestic relations office, or Title IV - D agency to enforce, modify, or clarify the medical support order.

(b) This subchapter does not limit the authority of the court to render or modify a medical support order containing a provision for payment of uninsured health expenses, health care costs, or health insurance premiums that are in addition to and inconsistent with this subchapter.

§ 154.192. Cancellation or Elimination of Insurance Coverage for Child

(a) Unless the employee or member ceases to be eligible for dependent coverage, or the employer has eliminated dependent health coverage for all of the employer's employees or members, the employer may not cancel or eliminate coverage of a child enrolled under this subchapter until the employer is provided satisfactory written evidence that:

(1) the court order or administrative order requiring the coverage is no longer in effect; or

(2) the child is enrolled in comparable health insurance coverage or will be enrolled in comparable coverage that will take effect not later than the effective date of the cancellation or elimination of the employer's coverage.

§ 158.001. Income Withholding; General Rule

In a proceeding in which periodic payments of child support are ordered, modified, or enforced, the court or the Title IV-D agency shall order that income be withheld from the disposable earnings of the obligor as provided by this chapter.

§ 158.002. Suspension Of Income Withholding

Except in a Title IV-D case, the court may provide, for good cause shown or on agreement of the parties, that the order withholding income need not be issued or delivered to an employer until:

(1) the obligor has been in arrears for an amount due for more than 30 days;

(2) the amount of the arrearages is an amount equal to or greater than the amount due for a one month period; or

(3) any other violation of the child support order has occurred.

§ 158.008. Priority of Withholding

An order or writ of withholding has priority over any garnishment, attachment, execution, or other assignment or order affecting disposable earnings.

§ 158.009. Maximum Amount Withheld From Earnings

An order or writ of withholding shall direct that any employer of the obligor withhold from the obligor's disposable earnings the amount specified up to a maximum amount of 50 percent of the obligor's disposable earnings.

§ 158.010. Order or Writ Binding on Employer Doing Business in State

An order or writ of withholding issued under this chapter and delivered to an employer doing business in this state is binding on the employer without regard to whether the obligor resides or works outside this state.

§ 158.202. Effective Date of and Duration of Withholding

An employer shall begin to withhold income in accordance with an order or writ of withholding not later than the first pay period following the date on which the order or writ was delivered to the employer and shall continue to withhold income as required by the order or writ as long as the obligor is employed by the employer.

§ 158.203. Remitting Withheld Payments

(a) The employer shall remit the amount to be withheld to the person or office named in the order or writ on each pay date. The payment must include the date on which the withholding occurred.

(b) For payments made by electronic funds transfer or electronic data interchange, the employer shall transmit the amount withheld not later than the second business day after the pay date.

(c) The employer shall include with each payment transmitted:

(1) the number assigned by the Title IV—D agency, if available, and the county identification number, if available;

(2) the name of the county or the county's federal information processing standard code;

(3) the cause number of the suit under which withholding is required;

(4) the payor's name and social security number; and

(5) the payee's name and, if available, social security number, unless the payment is transmitted by electronic funds transfer.

(d) In a case in which an obligor's income is subject to withholding, the employer shall remit the payment of child support directly to a local registry, the Title IV—D agency, or to the state disbursement unit.

§ 158.204. Employer May Deduct Fee From Earnings

An employer may deduct an administrative fee of not more than $10 each month from the obligor's disposable earnings in addition to the amount to be withheld as child support.

§ 158.206. Liability and Obligation of Employer for Payments

(a) An employer receiving an order or a writ of withholding under this chapter, including an order or writ directing that health insurance be provided to a child, who complies with the order or writ is not liable to the obligor for the amount of income withheld and paid as required by the order or writ.

(b) An employer receiving an order or writ of withholding who does not comply with the order or writ is liable:

(1) to the obligee for the amount not paid in compliance with the order or writ, including the amount the obligor is required to pay for health insurance under Chapter 154;

(2) to the obligor for:

(A) the amount withheld and not paid as required by the order or writ; and

(B) an amount equal to the interest that accrues under Section 157.265 on the amount withheld and not paid; and

(3) for reasonable attorney's fees and court costs.

§ 158.207. Employer Receiving More Than One Order or Writ

(a) An employer receiving two or more orders or writs for one obligor shall comply with each order or writ to the extent possible.

(b) If the total amount due under the orders or writs exceeds the maximum amount allowed to be withheld under Section 158.009, the employer shall pay an equal amount towards the current support in each order or writ until the employer has complied fully with each current support obligation and, thereafter, equal amounts on the arrearages until the employer has complied with each order or writ, or until the maximum total amount of allowed withholding is reached, whichever occurs first.

§ 158.208. Employer may Combine Amounts Withheld

An employer required to withhold from more than one obligor may combine the amounts withheld and make a single payment to each agency designated if the employer separately identifies the amount of the payment that is attributable to each obligor.

§ 158.209. Employer's Penalty for Discriminatory Hiring or Discharge

(a) An employer may not use an order or writ of withholding as grounds in whole or part for the termination of employment or for any other disciplinary action against an employee.

(b) An employer may not refuse to hire an employee because of an order or writ of withholding.

(c) If an employer intentionally discharges an employee in violation of this section, the employer continues to be liable to the employee for current wages and other benefits and for reasonable attorney's fees and court costs incurred in enforcing the employee's rights as provided in this section.

(d) An action under this section may be brought by the employee, a friend of the court, the domestic relations office, or the Title IV-D agency.

§ 158.210. Fine for Noncompliance

(a) In addition to the civil remedies provided by this subchapter or any other remedy provided by law, an employer who knowingly violates the provisions of this chapter may be subject to a fine not to exceed $200 for each occurrence in which the employer fails to:

(1) withhold income for child support as instructed in an order or writ issued under this chapter; or

(2) remit withheld income within the time required by Section 158.203 to the payee identified in the order or writ or to the state disbursement unit.

(b) A fine recovered under this section shall be paid to the county in which the obligee resides and shall be used by the county to improve child support services.

§ 158.211. Notice of Termination of Employment and of New Employment

(a) If an obligor terminates employment with an employer who has been withholding income, both the obligor and the employer shall notify the court or the Title IV—D agency and the obligee of that fact not later than the seventh day after the date employment terminated and shall provide the obligor's last known address and the name and address of the obligor's new employer, if known.

(b) The obligor has a continuing duty to inform any subsequent employer of the order or writ of withholding after obtaining employment.